TOURING CAR RACING
IN AUSTRALIA

BOOK TWO: 1981-1985

BY DEREK RAWSON
WITH CONTRIBUTIONS FROM FELLOW TEAM MEMBERS

First published as Print on Demand paperback by IngramSpark Dec. 2021
Revision two, July 2022

Text © Derek Rawson 2020

ISBN: 978-0-6451661-2-5

Copyright is claimed for this book as a whole. Please feel free however to quote or use sections of text for your own purposes. Creating this book has been more a labour of love than a money making exercise, its purpose to record the story of the Nissan Bluebird Turbo race cars and the EXA Turbo racer from the perspective of the team of guys who developed them. I've also wanted to offer our team's perspectives on the actors involved and to some extent correct stories I've read in print and online, particularly in recent years via social media – records should always be set straight.

Please feel free to offer corrections or additions if you feel you have contradicting or additional information that you think should be disclosed or corrected.

Please contact me via email: djr@pobox.com

 A catalogue record for this book is available from the National Library of Australia

Cover images
Top panel from left:
    Fury/Suffern 1981 Castrol International Rally, Datsun Stanza
    Fred Gibson 1983 approaching ARCO corner at Sandown Park
    George Fury with Bluebird #3 and his 1984 Bathurst pole trophy
    George Fury pitstop full dress rehearsal, 1984 Bathurst
    Christine Gibson in the EXA Turbo. 1983 Castrol 400 at Sandown
Bottom: Team photo taken at Sandown September 1983.
From left, George Fury, George Smith, Jamie Drummond, Steve Kaitler, Derek Rawson, Howard Marsden, Christine Gibson, Ian Walburn, Barry Bray, Trevor Jones, Fred Gibson, John French, Kevin King, Dennis Watson, Peter Anderson, Wyn Ellery. (Gary Scott and Bob Muir would fill the drivers' rank for Bathurst that year.)

"With the re-branding of the company in Australia from Datsun to Nissan, Howard Marsden orchestrated a move into Australian Group C Touring Car racing with the turbo Bluebird. George Fury and Fred Gibson took the wheel and although championship and Bathurst wins eluded Nissan, race wins and the famed 1984 pole position at Mount Panorama in the final year of the formula were precursors to significant success in following years."

— adapted from an article on Speedcafe.com

Regarding the photos used to illustrate this book.

I have amassed an extensive collection of photos in the 40 intervening years since we began Nissan's touring car racing program, some taken by myself, many more by other team members, and some commissioned by Nissan for publicity. Others turned up in various Google searches and some others I found in various motorsport journals and magazines, particularly the Australian Motor Racing Yearbooks of the time, old Auto Action mags, and retrospective features in Muscle Car Magazine and the like.

Another valuable source has been Bathurst specialist photographer Warren Hawkless. Wazza befriended George Fury and sent him prints of all the photos that featured him. George lent me his album for this project and I was excited at the prospect of including many of Wazza's pics. When I recently contacted him seeking permission to include these in the book, he very generously said to go for it and that he was very much looking forward to seeing the finished product. Thanks mate, I hope you enjoy seeing them all in print again.

Aaron Noonan of AN1 Media has, over the years, acquired several libraries of motorsport images from retiring photographers and has proven both a valuable souce of photos and guide on the legal use of images for this project.

Other than the above, I regret I didn't make more of an effort to keep the source information with many of the pics I dug up. If you wish to claim ownership of a particular image or images, please contact me, I'll be more than happy to add source acknowledgements for subsequent printings and/or to come to some mutually acceptable arrangement.

CONTENTS

About the Author vi
The Back Story 1
Acknowlegements 3
The Team 5
Introduction: Datsuns at Bathurst – The Early Years
        by Roger Bonhomme 30
Preface 33
The Story
    1981 35
    1982 47
    1983 73
    1984 119
    1985 153
Development 157
    Front suspension 158
    Body work 161
    Rear suspension 163
    Gearbox & Final drive 165
    Brakes 166
    Wheels & Tyres 167
    Engine & Turbocharger 169
    EXA 183
Addendums
    Racing venues 187
    Cars' History 193
    Spreadsheet of Cars, Drivers & Events 199
Personal thanks 201

ABOUT THE AUTHOR

By age 16, after disinterestedly meandering my way through year 10 at a pretty expensive Melbourne school, all I really wanted to do was get an apprenticeship as a motor mechanic.

My father, who'd already made a significant investment in my eduction, wasn't having any of it though and managed to keep me pedalling, albeit without much of a grip on the handlebars. All of my own time was spent in our family garage.

If I could have my time over again I'd be afraid to do anything differently in the worry that any slight change might send me off in some different direction and I'd have missed a grand, thirteen-year adventure with Nissan Motor Co. I really would have liked to have done an engineering degree though…

By dint of enthusiasm, interest and dedication I went from a young guy servicing rally cars for friends to developing engines to compete with Cosworth BDGs in works Ford Escorts and play in a team that won multiple Australian Rally Championships and multiple Southern Cross International Rallies.

Howard Marsden demonstrated a remarkable faith in his rally team and took us all on the journey into Touring Car racing when many would have sought out experienced replacements. Maybe he couldn't be bothered with the search, I have no idea and who knew what his motivations were, certainly not me, he was still largely a mystery after 10 years. I have a lot to be thankful for.

When my motorsport career came to a close in 1987 I gradually transistioned into computers and ended up spending the largest chunk of my working life repairing and supporting Apple Mac computers.

I do hope you enjoy my story of our racing exploits with Nissan.

Passing some waiting time with Wayne Manken at Calder Motor Raceway, early 1983.

TEAM BACK STORY

If you've come to this book via its companion, *"The Datsun Rally Team in Australia, 1974-1981"* you'll know that Nissan's touring car racing efforts in the early nineteen eighties grew from a team that had become used to success. Following its corporatisation at the end of 1975, our team won the Australian Rally Championship in 1976, '77, '79, '80 and '81 and Australia's premier rallying event, the Southern Cross International, in 1977, '78 '79 and '80.

Our Capitain Howard Marsden, whose resumé when he took on our team already boasted many successes in motorsport, significantly enhanced his reputation during this period.

Nissan Motor Co., Japan already had a strong record of motorsport success when it's Australian subsidiary took over the local team (which had until then been run from Bruce Wilkinson's Datsun dealership). From the beginning until 1979 our team's task was to localise and improve an already good product but from then on we were trusted to build cars from the ground up.

When we launched into the Group C Bluebird Turbo touring car project, we were told, and certainly at the beginning believed, we were aiming at success in a minor class but this, almost immediately, proved to be too easy.

Breaching the gap to dominate the outright category though, would prove to be something else. If only we'd had one more year…

Email me if you'd like to obtain a copy of the prequel.

ACKNOWLEDGEMENTS

I'd firstly like to acknowledge and thank Howard Marsden who, from 1976, led Nissan's motor sport team for the nine years we rallied and then raced, until he gave the team to his friend Fred Gibson in 1985. He kept faith in me as I continued to grow into my role. I wish he were still with us.

Secondly, the hero who made all our long hours and efforts worthwhile. George Fury had achieved every success available to him in rallying for Datsun before progressing to circuit racing in 1981. After a very short apprenticeship under Gibson, he mastered the challenging Turbo Bluebird, easily eclipsing Fred. He graduated from being co-driver in car #55 in position 43 on the grid at the 1981 James Hardie 1000, to coming within a trice of winning the 1983 Touring Car Championship and then captured pole position with an eight-year, record-holding time at the 1984 James Hardie (Bathurst) 1000.

Thirdly, my heroic core teammates with whom I shared these four amazing years (some of whom had shared a segment of the foregoing rallying adventures) listed here in the chronological order they joined the team.

    1976   Jamie Drummond (dec)
    1979   Peter Anderson
    1980   George Smith
    1982   Dennis Watson
    1982   Barry Bray

Fourthly, Mr Sasamoto, chief engineer and vice president of Nissan Motor Co. Australia, who in 1975 thought I should be the first mechanic in his just corporatised Datsun Rally Team. Thanks so much, Sas, you changed my life.

Introducing THE TEAM

in order of their appearance on stage.

GEORGE FURY

"I am really pleased to have been asked to contribute to this book and I have enjoyed the reminiscing.

I reckon my life has been a fortunate one in all ways and a large part of it was in motorsport.

When I was fourteen our family of four came to Australia as refugees, and looking back from that point, my life seemed to lead me to both motorsport and a life on the land.

Once I decided to give motorsport a go, it took some years to be able to fund my start in rallying, but soon after, luck led me to a drive in the Southern Cross Rally with the Datsun Rally Team where I met Derek. So it seems that Derek and I began our motorsport careers about the same time, give or take.

Shortly after, my wife Margi and I became partners on a farm with Margi's sister Pam and her husband Graeme. Amazingly this all ended up forming a great balance between working on the land and the competition of motorsport.

Part of Datsun's ambition at the time was to achieve victory in the annual Southern Cross International Rally. The Company was seriously invested in this project and had been trying to win for some years. Early in 1976, just after the Rally Team was corporatized, Howard Marsden joined us as team manager. Towards the end of the seventies the rally team, and Monty and I were able to help the company to finally achieve the goal of winning the 'Cross'. There was much celebration.

The seventies was a magnificent era in Australian rallying and I felt very lucky to be involved professionally as a works driver.

Everything in life fluctuates though – just like cattle prices – and by the end of the decade rallying had lost impetus and car manufacturer supported rallying was reaching its end.

In early 1980 Nissan Motor Co. head office in Japan decided to drop the Datsun name and instead just call its cars 'Nissan'. Fortunately for our rally team, Howard Marsden hatched the idea of promoting the Datsun to Nissan name change in Australia through participation in touring car racing. His plans involved keeping our successful team together and turning it into a race team. He was able to sell this idea to the management of Nissan Motor Co. Australia.

So, luckily for me and the boys in the workshop, our careers did not finish with rallying and we went on to compete on racetracks around Australia. Sadly though, as a navigator was no longer required, it was the end of my great partnership with Monty Suffern, one that had endured for all those years in the rally car. He was my best friend as well as my teammate from the beginning to the end of our rallying careers. To my mind, Monty remains the best navigator/co-driver Australian Rallying has had, at least in my time.

Plans were formed on how to go about achieving our race/rally transition. Initially my involvement in this consisted of discussing all the possibilities with Howard while we drove what were often long miles home after a rally or from a testing session.

It turned out that Howard had a lot of confidence in his mechanics' abilities, and in mine for that matter, to learn a new discipline. He told me he was sure I could, at the age of 40, adapt to driving on the racetrack.

He also knew though that we'd need someone with experience and knowledge of circuit racing as we didn't collectively know all that much about it. Howard asked Fred Gibson, with whom he'd worked at Ford in the early Falcon racing days, to be involved and to help start the team on the new path.

I remember asking Howard why he chose me to drive the Bluebird, rather than an established circuit racer. He said he liked the idea of keeping the rally team together. He also said he respected many of my driving attributes. Howard seemed to have no fear when I drove him in fog, with the cruise control set at 100kph. Nor did he turn a hair when we crashed while testing at Mount Slide. Just part of the deal…

As an introduction to circuit racing I drove in some sports sedan races in a track modified rally car. It was invaluable experience for me, especially because I lacked experience in close racing and racecraft.

So, the Bluebird Turbo came on the scene as the promotional tool to turn Datsun into Nissan in the eyes of the public. It was a huge learning curve for all team members.

My experience in rally car testing in the development of our Stanzas becoming competitive with the Ford Works Escort BDA, the yardstick at the time, proved invaluable. Testing on the race track followed on naturally and Fred's track experience was important at the start of the journey.

It was fortunate too that Margi was interested and able to do the lap timing for the team during testing and at the races. Bear in mind that in those days electronic timing was in its infancy and the teams still had to provide their own timers. In fact there were some occasions when Margi and Jillie Johnson had to give their timing data to the official timers to help them out.

There were a number of development issues involved in turning the Bluebird road car into a race car.

Derek was the engine man and he solved all the problems that surfaced, eventually ending up with a totally reliable engine. The regulations though required that the turbocharger retain its standard dimensions. A turbocharger designed for a 140bhp road going engine was required to pump enough air to make 350bhp to go racing. Sadly this proved near impossible to achieve with reliability until we were allowed some leeway with the turbocharger near the end of the Bluebird's program.

The chassis had to be modified to go racing. This was mainly handled by George Smith, Jamie Drummond and Pete Anderson. They put a lot of effort into the required suspension tuning and we spent a lot of time and effort testing on various tracks.

At the end of the Bluebird's development we finished up with a great handling race car, probably the best I have driven. I think this is because the team had taken advantage of all the freedoms in the rules allowed at the time regarding suspension development.

Most memorable for me, early on, was breaking rear stub axles. This meant a lost rear wheel while under cornering load. Luckily none of these ended in a major accident. We probably broke four before the problem was overcome.

I reckon the team did a great job during this Bluebird era as a lot of the time they made important decisions themselves when

Howard proved hard to find, dealing with his other job at company headquarters.

We'd learned a lot. It was hard and a pity when it was all over. We had a bond between us that started in the rally days and we worked well together on the Bluebird – enthusiasm and dedication never waned.

As the Bluebird days ended and the Nissan Skyline race car took its place, Howard stepped back from the race team and Fred Gibson took over the management and ownership, with outside sponsorship, something Datsun/Nissan had always largely avoided.

We had some great successes in Touring Car Racing with the Bluebird, despite it being the underdog against the V8 and rotary engined cars. I enjoyed those days immensely and was disappointed when they had to end.

But now the next page in life was turned for us all."

We can't let such humility be the sum of what this book says about George though, so I wish to add:

With an already impressive record of success in rallying, George arrived in my life a ready-made hero. From 1973 when I watched him in my first experience of the Southern Cross Rally and especially after he took me for a ride in the works Datsun 710 at Mt Slide[1] in 1976, he became a figure of awe which was enhanced somewhat by his slight aloofness, a by-product of his characteristic shyness. He would be a key character in my life for the ensuing ten years.

A talented, practical engineer, great thinker, laser focussed and naturally gifted driver, he'd have been at the top of any rally team manager's wish list. Thanks are due to Bruce Wilkinson who recognised his talent and gave him the break he needed to burst onto the national rally scene and quickly lock-in his place. George became part of the package requisitioned by Nissan Australia late in 1975.

He was an excellent development driver, able to give Howard and our crew not only clear feedback when testing but, more often than not, also practical suggestions to allow us to move forward.

Thinking about how to characterise him, 'thoughtful' comes immediately to mind. If he wasn't driving he'd most likely be found contemplating the issue de jour, often scribbling notes in his little

---

1   Near Toolangi, north east of Melbourne where we used to test.

book – a constant companion. He was quite shy and, it seemed to me, self conscious, which in my mind, was rather at odds with his fierce determination to do well. When he did, he never looked very comfortable on the podium or on a stage receiving a trophy. He had an endearing smile but shared it a little too sparingly.

He seemed to shun the limelight and seemed happier to be one of the boys than having to pander to the media, the sponsors, or even the other crews, he was our hero and he appeared to enjoy being amongst us. How bloody brilliant.

With George's enthusiastic support, Howard decided to put his and the company's faith in him for the ensuing years of circuit racing with the Turbo Bluebird. A short period of transition followed as he adapted his driving style and car setup and become one of the undisputed 'guns' on the Australian touring car scene.

Richard Power, an early Nissan marketing department go between, liaising with Datsun Race and Rally Teams, has a way with words and says so eloquently of George: *"He was mostly a quiet, smiley, somewhat unflappable yet steely impatient hyper speedster on any surface, rally or race. …George could drive at the max but still with meccanico simpatico to preserve the car."*

As most readers will probably know, George went on to successfully race Group A Nissan Skylines in the privatised Nissan team under Fred Gibson and then Group A BMWs, Ford Sierras and even a Mitsubishi Galant VR4.

He returned to rallying with some success in 1990 but was pretty much done with professional motorsport by 1991, redoubling his efforts on their farm beside the Murray River.

He and Margi retired around 2020 and now live in Gippsland's Korumburra.

Belts on and tight – check…
Fury at ATCC round Sandown 1984

HOWARD MARSDEN

Howard was a true English gentleman complete with posh English accent. He had a knack of being able to tell people just what they wanted to hear, in a very friendly and never condescending sounding manner. He could keep this up until he'd promised his way into a corner and then, if needs be, he could be quite blunt. I'm quite sure many of those who had dealings with him would have preferred to skip the preliminaries and get straight to blunt.

Working under Howard could be very frustrating until, late in the day, we finally accepted we couldn't depend on him doing what he said he'd do, and we'd learned 'if it was to be – it was up to me'.

That off my chest, we were truly blessed to be captained by Howard – I shudder to contemplate how different an experience it would have been had Harry Firth accepted that role – which was first offered to him.

Howard's contract with Nissan came with the senior executive position of Product Evaluation Manager and he had a nice office and (mercifully) a very efficient secretary in Nissan Australia's head office on Frankston-Dandenong Road, South Dandenong. As he was quoted in the media, *"Datsun is the only company which has a direct link from our motorsport program back into the company."* Also though, *"My motorsport activities are a relatively small part of my job"*.

His executive role must have kept him reasonably busy, he had several work trips to Japan for instance. Apart from when we were away on events or out testing, which he seldom missed, particularly as the years went by, we saw little of him. In the latter years of touring car racing I estimate that on average he'd pay us a visit at the workshop something less than once per fortnight and usually not stay very long.

Richard Power's[2] impression: *An English gentleman of impeccably diplomatic manner who somehow found himself cornered in the world of motorsport. He used to respond to entreaties as to how to get into*

---

2   Richard worked for Graham Currie in Nissan's Public Relations Department at Head Office. He was a keen motorsport competitor and enthusiast, helped out on many events and has a snazzy way with words.

motorsport by asking how could he get out of it. Howard was a strategic thinker with an unerring eye to leveraging the sport for marketing effect.

Howard was a darling to the motoring media and our team's many fans but he could be a major frustration to those he worked for and to those of us who depended upon him.

There were many times over the years that we the 'hands on' got to a stage of needing guidance and for decisions to be made, and we'd request a face-to-face. He'd schedule a meeting at his office and, at the appropriate time, we'd get cleaned up and drive up there only to find he was not there and his secretary had no idea where he was. We'd wait a while and then head back to work. On occasions when he'd turn up at the workshop, we'd all sit down with a coffee (or tea of course in his case). We'd spend a half hour or more together and we'd feel heard, appeased and even satisfied but, on getting back to the problems at hand, realise we'd received no relevant decisions and few relevant pearls of wisdom. Howard was master at this. He seemed to have complete faith that passionate and dedicated people would make good choices and work their way though any problem that arose – and we usually did.

On one occasion we had his Nissan Skyline at the workshop for some work (fitting the giant pump-up antenna or something) and one of us discovered a cheque on the rear floor, dirty footprints and all. It was for $10,000, from Total Oil, made out to Nissan Motor Co., dated some months prior. Knowing it would be an embarrassment if we drew his attention to it, we left it where we found it. And there it stayed for months longer. We always had a laugh when one of us noticed it hadn't moved when next we saw the car. Total must have rung eventually to say hey, you know last year's sponsorship cheque…

Under Harry Firth[3], development would likely have proceeded at a faster rate, but we workers would not have had to think and problem solve, we'd not have been empowered. I can now thank Howard's memory for this great gift and wish I'd done so as we were parting ways. At the time though, I was too embittered in frustration.

On events though, Howard was usually brilliant. On the Southern Cross Internationals of 1978, '79 and '80 which we won with Stanzas, he had a fairly large team to manage and co-ordinate. We service crews, got by with little sleep over the four days of the event. Howard though, had even less, as each morning, before we jumped in the vans to head

---

3   first offered the role by Mr Sasamoto

out, we were each handed a comprehensive set of instructions and maps covering the mountainous terrain being used for the coming division. On these were marked the competitor's route and the suggested route for us to access our assigned stage ends throughout the forests. Howard and Rex Muldoon, or later, Howard and Phil Rainer, would have been up earlier, after going to bed later, to plan the following night's service activities – and it all worked, almost without a hitch.

Howard and Rex/Phil would head out into the forests in the 2-door orange Skyline with its enormous pump-up VHF aerial mounted astern. They'd sussed out the highest accessible spots to create useable radio comms for the territory in use that night, in order to be able to direct and resolve issues arising. We all took pride in this endeavour and its success.

At rallies and race meetings, when we needed to be focused on the cars, HM was always on hand to distract and sweet-talk the ever-present journos. Thank you Howard. I don't know how but I think you actually enjoyed this role. It was always amusing to see what turned up in Auto Action a week or so later. (It's proved frustrating for me in researching for these books though – I've had to keep asking myself, was this really what happened?)

Howard's serious and professional nature was a good match for lead driver George Fury and they enjoyed an enduring and successful relationship. Navigator Monty Suffern's quiet and methodical nature also fitted right in. The success the rally team enjoyed was due in no small part to this great 3-way partnership.

Another episode that illustrates Howard's 'management style' centres on our post rally celebrations after a successful Australian Rally Championship event in Western Australia. We were staying in a very nice, 10-story hotel in Perth CBD and they had some waste-high earthenware pots in the lift foyers. After a few too many beers downed by aforementioned service crew, it seemed like a humorous idea to put these pots in the lift and send them down to reception. First one then four or five. There was much rather drunken hilarity.

After returning to Melbourne, at a debriefing meeting at our workshop, Howard produced a bill from the hotel for the replacement of one four-foot earthenware vase. "Do you boys know anything about this?" Four blank guileless faces were our reply. "OK, well I'll just mark this to be paid," was his knowing response. Things needed to be far more serious before he'd be willing to confront. We did hear several times in following years though, that "You boys are becoming very expensive."

A couple of years later, we were testing a revamped rear suspension on the Bluebird at Calder Raceway and had some visiting Japanese in attendance. Jamie was standing at the front of the Bluebird racer, while at the rear, Howard was regaling the Japanese with his 'prodigious engineering skills'. In response to an unheard question, Howard said it had been he who'd designed the rear suspension. Poor Jamie came as close as he ever had to the top of his head coming off – I swear we could see steam coming out of his ears. Had HM been asked about this later (and there's a good possibility he was as Jamie's wrath did not subside quickly), Howard would have had a good and almost convincing response.

Howard's wife, Christine, is the most lovely and charming person you'd ever hope to meet. Sadly we saw her infrequently. Howard's life away from work was unfortunately seldom shared with us. I choose to think that this was a factor of his character rather than a deliberate choice to exclude the unwashed from his extra curricular life, but I'm not completely sure about this. I did a stint at Dick Johnson Racing after my time at Nissan. Dick was one of the boys – after-work beers and occasional parties at his house were part of the scene. A very different experience to working for Howard. At time of writing, Dick is still with us and Howard is not. I wish for all our sakes that he'd been better at sharing his stresses and frustrations – bottling this stuff up often causes it to eat one up from inside, which is what led to him being taken from us.

There very often seemed to be some sort of deal going on in the background, often involving tyres or suspension struts or brakes or what have you. When we were at Braeside, someone would turn up at the workshop and tell us they'd come to pick up the tyres, or whatever, that Howard had organised. We'd know nothing about it so we'd have to ring head office to get the "oh yes, just give him four used 195/14s" or whatever it happened to be. Before that, at South Melbourne, probably because there were Nissan execs stationed there, these 'deals' would involve one of us dropping off components to a certain associated premises in Brighton after hours.

I only discovered a few years ago that as part of the arrangement whereby the rally team was removed from Wilkinson at Hartwell and installed at South Melbourne under Marsden, all used components and tyres from the team would be disposed of through Wilkinson's DatsunSport business which had the franchise to sell Nissan competition parts in

Australia. Bruce felt aggrieved when after a year of so he'd received zilch from the team and he apparently complained to Nissan management. When confronted, Howard stated bluntly that no, that wasn't going to happen. Apparently no one called him to account and Howard continued to use parts and tyres as currency for his own purposes – partly I'm sure though to 'grease the wheels' with people he needed on-side.

Some time around 1977 Howard approached me with a business proposal involving himself, John Armitage and myself. The plan involved John selling used rally bits from a shop front, I would operate a workshop behind it, fitting the parts and doing other mods and Howard would, I guess, grease the wheels. We got as far as locating a premises in Canterbury before it all fell though – thank God! I don't remember why or why it was never spoken about again and sadly I have no way to find out as I'm the last man standing, so to speak. It was just another slice of fortuitous luck on my journey with Nissan and I'm so happy everything worked out as it did.

When Howard left Nissan early in 1985, Paul Beranger, who took over his role, found he needed to recover eleven Nissan vehicles that Howard had 'lent' to people all over the country. I gather Paul had fairly limited success.

I have no axe to grind. Howard treated me very well, forgave my shortcomings and allowed me the opportunity to learn an enormous amount. I just don't want to let slip the opportunity to 'balance the books' a little. Howard was not the omniscient God he was portrayed as by the motoring journalists of the day, nor the commentators on Facebook in more recent times. He was a guy who had a very clever knack of being able to give credit where it was due while giving the impression he was really just being magnanimous. I reckon Howard enjoyed the game he often played of offering maybe four parts truth, three parts invention to cover what he didn't know, and the rest just playful rubbish in order just to play with you.

Recently there was a retrospective article published in a glossy monthly and written by a journalist who's been around since our rallying days and who gave our team great mirth by how much of this 'Howie speak' he would absorb and what he wrote subsequently. A myth has developed over the years about the Nissan Bluebird Turbo's alleged facility to enable boost adjustment by the driver (contrary to the rules of the day). Some 16 years after HM's passing, this journalist was convinced of the truth of a 'confession' from Howard that this was achieved by pulling the ashtray out to increase boost and pushing it back to reduce it. One of the funniest thing I ever read. Thanks Howard, you keep on giving.

Howard succumbed to a seven month battle with stomach cancer in August 2003 and was farewelled by a capacity crowd in the main room at the Sofitel Hotel in Collins Street, Melbourne. The event was attended by the who's who of Australian motorsport.

For a period, pulling the ashtray out would at least provide *access* to a boost controller.

JAMIE DRUMMOND

Born 1955 Jamie was a country boy from Walwa in Victoria, just up-river a bit and on the other side of the Murray from George Fury's farm at Talmalmo. Truly magnificent country.

He'd done his motor mechanics apprenticeship in Albury and had come to the notice of Fury some time in 1975. Captivated by his general enthusiasm (I'd suggest) George would have recommended him to Howard as a suitable young addition to our team and he showed up in Melbourne as we were moving the rally team to the much larger premises at Braeside in Melbourne's south east at the end of 1975. We became great mates immediately. Here are some details extracted from emails between us (with only minor edits for clarity) in the last months before his passing:

"When I had my interview with Howard early in 1975, he offered me 4 different jobs – Bob Jane, Allan Moffat, Frank Gardner and Nissan. He gave me one month to decide!

"I left my job in Albury in middle of 1975 and moved to Nth Dandenong, in SE suburbs of Melbourne. I travelled into South Melbourne every day for a few months. Howard got me a job just servicing cars there. That's where I first met you. He told me it might take a little time before I could join the Rally Team because of the planned move out to Braeside etc. I was like a deer in the headlights and was hanging on his every word but I remember thinking: Is this really going to happen? I got the impression he was making it up as he spoke. So I asked him if I could get a job closer to Dandenong. He agreed and got me a job at an Ampol service station in Mentone!! He kept saying I couldn't start with the rally team full time. I think he was stringing me along for a while.

"I'd work at Mentone then drive in to South Melbourne after hours and help you pack up for the move. You were the only one there, I've no idea where Barry [Nelson] was. And then after a few months Howard told me that my full time employment had been approved and I started with you at Braeside!"

I really don't think I would have been employed if it wasn't for

George F and also me being super keen helping and learning at night after work!

I wouldn't change a thing though! Except maybe losing my licence for 2 and a half years... [I'll spare you, and his memory, the details]

Jamie was a great addition to our team, hard working, enthusiastic and a straight shooter – he knew what a spade was for and he knew what to call it. And if the job needed spade work he was the first to grab a spade. This was in the days before we had adopted our specialties, when it was all hands on deck to be ready for the next event, whatever that took.

The first of our 6-cyl E20 service vans became his. He drove it with enthusiasm, as with everything, and looking back, you'd have to say that, in the end, he'd been pretty lucky to make it to 64 years. More than one team mate applied to Howard for a transfer after being assigned to team up with him in 'his' E20.

This and the rallying book was to have been a joint project between the two of us. He had a good memory (well, better than mine anyway) and we thought we could create a terrific book combining our talents. As it turned out I got very little from Jamie before we lost him[4]. If only I'd attacked the project with the same vigour Jamie was known for...

"I've got a good memory! And there's a lot more great times I can reflect on! I think you and I should write a book about our time at Nissan Motor Sport! I'll drag up the memories and you can write and configure the book! It would be a best seller! We have plenty of characters to choose from!"

---

4   On Saturday June 12, 2020 Jamie, driving his recently acquired FJ Holden, was stopped waiting to turn right into the Wangaratta (Vic) Airport when a Nissan Navara barrelled into the back of his car, instantly killing both he and his engineer friend. R.I.P. mate, it would have been terrific to have launched this book with you.

PETER ANDERSON

Pete Anderson and I had, in our early 20s, belonged to the Sportscar Owners Club of Victoria (SOCV) and used to go racing Sprites and MGs at club meetings. We'd lost contact for a while afterwards but when our fledgling Nissan race team was in need a full time welder/fabricator at the beginning of 1981, thankfully Pete was still around and available. It was great to be reacquainted and working together.

Pete had been a champion sailor in his teens and had later turned his hand to repairing boat fittings and fabricating components and accessories. No welding or fabrication job was beyond him it seemed, he took the quality of our locally-built 1980 Stanza rally car to a whole other level and this carried forward into the Bluebirds. We were proud to roll them off the trailer or out of our transporter and display the workmanship.

When Jamie lost his driver's licence for two and a half years, Pete drove him to and from work every day. Jamie credited him with saving his career.

Pete left Melbourne after the motorsport days had passed to return to his roots – starting a boating oriented fabricating business in Queensland's Airlie Beach. During this time he also contracted to Dennis Watson's and George Smith's Dencar Pty Ltd, fabricating front cross members and other components for the Holden Racing Team's body shells (and most of the privateer's of the time) being produced at Dencar.

'Real soon now' he'll get onto finishing his beautiful trimaran sail boat and finally do some cruising around the Whitsundays.

He and vivacious and steadfast partner Rhonda, have created a tropical paradise in seven acres of rain forest just west of Airlie Beach. They enjoy it still.

GEORGE SMITH

Another Tasmanian who'd struck out for the mainland with his child bride, George Smith was a part of Colin Bond's Ford Rally Team when we met him in 1977. He'd been fairly seriously burned in a pit lane fire with Allan Moffat's Falcon at Bathurst in 1978 but made a full recovery. I seem to remember that, at the end of 1979 he was disgruntled at Bondy's and was keen for a new challenge. So, being one man short after Pete Davis' departure, we approached George and he jumped at the opportunity. He relocated the family, wife Jan, seven year-old daughter Angie, Peter, two and Julianne, nine months, from Sydney to Dingley, not far from our workshop at Braeside.

With his racing experience he'd seen the better build quality of the race-cars of the time and, with a budget to work with, set about raising the standard of our Stanza's fabrication and presentation. The new Stanza we built from a body shell early in 1980 quickly reflected his and Peter Anderson's workmanship. I think it would be no exaggeration to say George taught us how to spend Nissan's money, something he had a flair for and took pretty seriously once we began racing.

A bit of a larrikin, George loved a drink after work and though I jest a little, he took relish in captaining the team in that regard, finding every chance to knock back a few on the company's dime. I reckon I'd have been able to remember quite a bit more of our years together had I not gotten tangled in all that. "You boys are becoming very expensive", we heard more than once from the guy who ended up with the bills on his desk.

Rather than being put off by Jamie's driving, George encouraged his daredevil antics. How the two of them came out of all that unscathed, mystifies me.

In the racing years, while I was ensconced in my spacious engine room at Healey Road, George had taken responsibility for the gearboxes, brakes and general fabrication as well as an unofficial workshop foreman role. I'd have to say that he could rightly claim more than his fair share of the successes we enjoyed with the turbo Bluebirds.

FRED GIBSON

Born 16 January, 1941, Sydney-based Gibson had begun racing in English sports cars but by 1967 had managed to gain a place in Harry Firth's Ford Falcon team where he had some success in the late '60s including a Gallagher 500 win at Bathurst after a lap recount that shifted Firth/Gibson above the Geoghegan's similar Falcon. Other than at his local circuits, Sydney's Amaroo and Oran Park, where he usually did well, the 1970s saw a drought of race results and his career drifted into the doldrums.

Probably due to his and Howard Marsden's histories with Ford, plus the Marsden/Gibson family relationships, Fred would have sprung to Howard's mind as a logical, experienced driver to build a team around when Nissan made the switch from rallying to circuit racing in 1981.

Quoting Fred from an interview he gave in more recent times: "[Marsden] *started that* [circuit racing] *program and asked me if I would be the driver with George and teach him how to drive a bitumen car which I did at Oran Park every week for weeks and weeks to get him to drive it and stop him flicking it (the tail of the car) everywhere!*

"That's how the Nissan thing started with Bluebird and helping George achieve what he achieved and it went on from there."

Yes, well, weeks and weeks? I do not think so. Anyway, apparently Fred did a way too good job and next thing you know he was over-shadowed and found himself very often making excuses for his performances.

This did not endear him to the team and Howard's continued failure to acknowledge Fred's shortcomings, organising instead for him to compete in his favoured back yard circuits, led to rifts in the team.

Even this though failed to provide shelter for his faltering racing career. The 1983 AMSCAR Series at Amaroo Park for instance should have provided Nissan valuable TV coverage, competing as he was against the second level touring car teams, but instead he could only manage to win one round of the four weekend series, and that less than convincingly. The series was dominated by a Mazda RX7 privateer team.

So, with Fred blaming our Melbourne-based operation for budget overspends, and sometimes his poor performances, our 1983 efforts were split and somewhat duplicated, with him running a second team out of his Sydney-based 'Road and Track' business.

Fred retired from driving at the end of 1983. In his words:

"*I decided to retire at Oran Park while qualifying the Bluebird* [13th with Fury on pole] *at a touring car round* [on May 28th].

"*To do a lap in the Bluebird it was full boost with new tyres… you had to nail the lap; as you didn't get a second chance, especially with the turbo engine and the Bluebird being so fragile. They wouldn't give you two laps of full boost and I remember coming through the Esses, weaving between a heap of cars on full throttle and thought, 'God strike me', I've just risked my life to do this lap. I shouldn't be doing this anymore and I should look at something else.*"

He did however, keep going till the end of the year, albeit at a reduced pace until, at Sandown in early September he managed 15th on the grid to Fury's fifth, and at Bathurst in October, with George on the front row, Fred could only qualify 18th. The full story will ensue.

Despite my less than glowing report of Fred Gibson as a driver, he is a genuine good bloke and I enjoy his occasional company. His character shines through in his considerable support in recent years of a rather frail Allan Moffat.

CHRISTINE GIBSON (née COLE)

Married to Fred through thick and thin since 1971 and a very talented race driver, Christine has nine major endurance races on her resumé. She drove a Mini in her first in 1968 then through Fiats, Falcons, Toranas, Alfa Romeos and Monaros to Nissan's EXA in 1983 and '84. Christine would have been the marketing department's dream choice for the little sports coupe.

For its first season the EXA proved difficult to drive due to its rather savage torque steer but she was not deterred and I think earned the respect of those who she raced against.

Christine is remembered as the First Lady of Bathurst.

DENNIS WATSON

Right from the beginning the job of organising wheels and tyres took significant man hours and it was soon evident we needed someone to take this on. Den had this role both with Allan Moffat's and Peter Brock's teams and had worked at both with George Smith. He was also a highly motivated and efficient Master panel beater, chassis repairer and painter, with fabrication skills second to none and when we discovered he was available it seemed like a no-brainer to immediately grab him and absorb these key roles in-house.

Den was a jovial character with a great laugh and was a big hit with the team. For George he was also a drinking buddy who could hold his own. With wife Carol they had a nice house with an in-ground pool on the highway at Hallam, ten minutes from our Healey Road workshop. We had some great pool parties there celebrating whatever needed celebrating at the time.

Den obtained his heavy duty articulated truck licence and became our truck driver once we took delivery of our Nissan UD prime-mover and pantec, adding yet another most valuable role in our team.

Den and George Smith went on to create 'Dencar', a specialist engineering business which constructed chassis and fabricated components for The Holden Racing Team and many others who raced Commodores in Australia between 1990 and 2005.

George is the only one of us who has stayed with racing, now working for long-time V8 Supercar racing, Team 18. Dennis still works as a fabricator but has turned his talents to caravans.

BARRY BRAY

Rather incongruously the manager of a printing company in Adelaide beforehand, but a racer and engineer at heart, Bazza had been a collaborator with our team since 1980. He'd built and was campaigning a beautiful 2-door Stanza Sports Sedan with a Lucas fuel injected LZ18 engine. When the opportunity to join us as a machinist arose in early 1982, Baz left the printing company and his glamorous wife Wendy, in Adelaide and moved to Melbourne.

Incredibly, as well as being able to machine up all the components asked of him, in 1983 he almost single-handedly built the EXA Turbo that Christine Gibson campaigned at Sandown, Amaroo and Mt Panorama in 1983–'84.

About this time too, he took up with Sally, one of the metallurgists at Nissan's Clayton manufacturing plant and through that relationship we got access to the many resources that were languishing there just waiting for something more interesting to do!

Baz now works for a company in Melbourne's southern suburbs that does engine development projects such as converting large diesels to run on gas with Motek engine management, battery powered London taxis, and all sorts of other interesting projects.

"Remember the morning Trevor Jones [one of Fred's boys] and I were having a little race to work in the E20s and the cops followed us to Healey Road? Howie had a few words with them and off they went in their new Nissan jackets." I didn't but it sure is great that a couple of us at least can still remember these gems.

Bazza's two Nissan Sports Sedans, the newer Nissan Gazelle here leading the Datsun Stanza 2-door.

MASAHIRO HASEMI

34 years old when he came to Australia for the James Hardie 1000 in 1981, Masahiro Hasemi had been a Nissan contracted driver since 1964 and by the time we met him had already achieved much success in Touring Car, Sports Car and Open Wheel racing including competing in the 1976 Formula One race in Japan. He had won Japan's 1980 Formula Two championship and went on to win his country's top Touring Car series in 1989, '91 and '92 with Nissan Skyline GT-Rs.

KAZUYOSHI HOSHINO

Known at home as 'The fastest man in Japan', Kazuyoshi Hoshino was a contemporary of Hasemi but two years his junior at a time when seniority was very much dictated by age in Asia. He'd become a Nissan contracted driver in 1969 and before he first came to Bathurst in 1981 he had competed in two Formula One Japanese Grand Prix and won three Japanese Top Formula Championships, 1975, '77 and '78.

Such was the Asia/Anglo divide at the time and despite my considerable interest in all things motorsport, neither of these obviously top-level drivers had so much as tickled the edges of my consciousness before I met them at our Braeside workshop in September 1981.

Hoshino would go on to win another three JTFCs in 1987, '90 and '93.

Both of these guys had very little English and none of our Aussie team had more than a few words of Japanese so communication proved difficult. There was no mistaking their intention, commitment, skill and daring though and we were all excited to see them re-appear in 1982.

THE JAPANESE ENGINEERS

There were at least four Japanese engineers who came out for our first two assaults on the James Hardie 1000. Each of them had also played a part in Nissan's assaults on the Southern Cross International Rally through the years and it was always great to welcome them back into our Aussie team.

'Gun' Kobayashi
Head Mechanic

Mr Gunn had first come out for the 1972 'Cross as a junior mechanic but by the time we were racing he'd risen to be the travelling team foreman. A great guy, he'd had enough international exposure to develop a good grasp of our strange language and even our Aussie sense of humour. He even had the good grace not to show too much distrust of the 'improvements' we made to their usually beyond-question Japanese engineering.

Heichan Kato
Engine Man

Kato san also first appeared with the 1972 crew and had always been the engine man. A little more reserved (maybe deferential?) than Gun san but also someone you'd want on your team. He wasn't all that keen on deviations to Japanese specifications though.

Saito san first appeared with the 1976 'Cross team and had correspondingly less English but was another great bloke and we usually got by.

Saito san
Mechanic

Iio san (like eeoh but Jamie re-christened him Mr One hundred and ten) was the Dunlop tyre technician assigned to Nissan Motorsport. A quite serious and reserved character, he too had been coming out since 1976.

There were others too who'd come before, notably Takashi Wakabayashi (international rally team boss), Mabu Kobayashi (first rally team foreman), Shinoda san (travelling team boss) and of course, Mr Hisashi Sasamoto, Chief Engineer and Vice President of Nissan Motor Co. Australia, who offered me a job with his newly corporatised Datsun Rally team.

Iio san
Dunlop Tyre techn'n

RON SAYER

Early in 1983, probably as a Howard initiative to reign in expenditure, a somewhat fierce-looking chap named Ron Sayer was installed in our Healey Road front office.

Ronnie was tasked with helping us with procurement and overseeing expenditure. He endured a lot of ribbing from us and we slowly turned him from a rather serious adversary to a kindly old uncle. Many scary invoices would have received the 'Ronnie Motorsport' stamp of approval before being nervously conveyed down the road to Howard's desk, where we collectively wished we could have been a fly on the wall at times.

Ron was often hovering around when we were working at race meetings and sometimes suffered the brunt of our frustrations during trying times. There was even the odd practical joke played. It was good to have had him there though.

I wish we could apologise for the hard times we gave him but I doubt very much he'd still be with us. If you do get to read this, Ron – sorry mate.

WYN ELLERIE & TREVOR JONES

Wyn and Trev were Fred Gibson's race mechanics from Road & Track in Sydney. For the best part of the racing years there was a complicated relationship with Gibson's Sydney-based operation but, like Fred, both Wyn and Trev were good guys and both came to Melbourne a few times to work with us at Healey Road.

Wyn at Healy Rd in 1982 and at right, between Pete and Jamie, is Trev – the only photo I've been able to find of him.

STEVE KAITLER

Like Jamie and George Fury, Steve Kaitler was from God's country up on the Murray River. He'd started a motor mechanic apprenticeship but then switched over to carpentering/building. When Les Collins offered him a job at Datrally Developments he jumped at the chance to come and work in the big city and spent three years there with Les mostly building engines, which was were we met him.

In 1982 we needed someone to make wooden crates to move our parts and equipment around the country so Steve enthusiastically came in after hours to get this handled. Then, as the load increased with our racing schedule, he joined us full time, helping me in the engine room and other assignments.

He tells me that Howard laid him off midway through 1984 in an effort to rein in costs. He returned to Corowa and started his own mechanical engineering business, later sub-contracting to Drummond Shock Absorbers among several other motorsport related projects.

IAN WALBURN

Wally Gator, as Baz Bray called him, had been working with Allan Moffat's Falcon team with Dennis Watson and Mick Webb. Around 1979 they helped build the first RX-7 Mazdas. Ian was a more than capable off-sider to Baz when the EXA project was taken on.

The Gator was a big strong guy too, just the ticket for lifting a 40 litre churn of fuel to plug into the back of a race car!

The best pic I could find of the Gator – a head above all but Howard Marsden.

GARY SCOTT

"Thinking about your request for thoughts and impressions of my Nissan Bluebird days there is one word that comes to mind... fantastic!

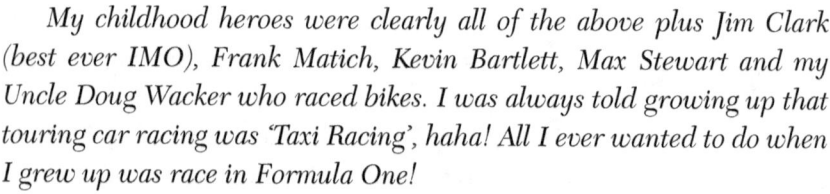

I was born into a well know Motor Racing family, my Dad was Glyn Scott who was a respected race driver and CAMS administrator until his untimely death in July, 1970 at Lakeside.

I grew up with the Geoghegans, Janes and Beecheys all staying at our home when they raced in Queensland. I clearly remember being my Dad's shadow from a young age.

My childhood heroes were clearly all of the above plus Jim Clark (best ever IMO), Frank Matich, Kevin Bartlett, Max Stewart and my Uncle Doug Wacker who raced bikes. I was always told growing up that touring car racing was 'Taxi Racing', haha! All I ever wanted to do when I grew up was race in Formula One!

Jumping through time I drove an Anglia Sports Sedan, Cheetah F3 (Australian F3 Champion for 1977) and Ralt F3 England 1978, then for both Dick Johnson (Falcon XC in 1979) and Peter Brock (Commodores 1981 and '82). Both were great guys and teams and I have many fabulous memories.

Early in 1983 Barry Tapsall recommended me to Howard Marsden as a potential driver and Howard called and invited me to join Nissan Motorsport. This was a great opportunity as I'd be a paid factory team driver making just the third professional driver in Australia after Jim Richards and George Fury!

The plan was to do Bathurst in '83 with George and then the Amaroo AMSCAR Series plus endurance races either with George or individually.

My first experience with the Bluebird was a test day at Oran Park, I was amazed at how different boost levels changed the car's dynamics so much! It was 'love at first drive' and I just couldn't get enough of driving the wheels off it. The team had developed it into a potent little rocket ship that you could take to the absolute limit and sometimes beyond with no vices! The Bluebird left a fabulous and lasting impression on me and it certainly earned its place in the Australian Touring Car history."

PART TIMERS

There were several part-time team members who came to events or just stepped up to help us out

From 1976 onward until the end of our race team, Victorian Rally Champs, **Chris and Simon Brown** were regular helpers willing to take on any job and they became great mates of our team.

Beginning in '79, **Dave Thompson** became a part-timer when we wanted to make wet sumps and other fabricated bits for the Stanzas. By the time we began the Bluebird project we had fabrication fully covered by Pete Anderson and George Smith but Dave was always on the short list to play a role if one popped up.

Simon Brown looking proud in team uniform at '82 Bathurst

Auto-elec., **Graeme (Jackie) Stewart**, who'd spent his early years at Ford Motor Co. Racing Division on their HO Falcon program under Howard.

He'd been keeping our alternators and starters in good shape for some years and joined the team intermittently, initially to build, and later modify, the Bluebirds' wiring looms – something I'd been responsible for until then – and also to lend a hand at Bathurst.

Graham (Jackie) Stewart picked out of the throng from the '84 pole photo

John Bailey was a Telstra engineer friend of George Fury's navigator, Monty, who provided us with electronic wizardry for all manner of projects though rallying and racing. One hellova nice and obliging bloke to have on any team.

Geoff Watson from Turbo Dynamics was really a service provider rather than a part timer but for a few months in the second half of 1984 our team must surely have been at least his largest customer and my job would have been so much more challenging without his considerable help.

Kevin King was a quiet achiever who joined us in 1983 for the Endurance Championship.

I'm sure there are others my faltering memory has failed to recall and I apologise. Please let me know if you're able to help complete the record – I can add names for the next printing.

Introduction

Datsuns at Bathurst – the early years
Contributed by Roger Bonhomme

The history of Nissan/Datsun car racing in Australia goes back more than 50 years. From 1966, Datsuns featured strongly in the annual Bathurst race for (almost) stock standard cars and for most years between '66 and '76, Datsuns were the cars to beat in Classes A an B, notching up 11 victories.

During the motor sporting era known as series production racing (with slight variations), Datsun cars proved successful because of their combination of reliability and relatively good performance. In Japan, Datsun had a strong racing team and for the 1966 Bathurst race, they entered two 1300 sedans for their works drivers Moto Kitamo/Kunimitsu Takahashi and Australian hotshots John Roxburgh/Doug Whiteford.

It proved a great idea as the pair of boxy-looking cars took out first and second in Class A for cars up to 1300cc. A year later the results were reversed with Roxburgh/Whiteford heading a team one-two over their Japanese teammates, Takahashi/Kitamo in newly released Datsun 1000s.

The saying in the motor trade "Win on Sunday, sell on Monday" appealed to George Denner, General Manager of Datsun Australia (later Nissan Australia). As a keen motorsport follower, he helped form the Datsun Racing Team with Roxburgh and Whiteford as lead drivers.

Later Roxburgh took over the running of the team for several years. He was the ideal man, having been first across the line in the 1960 Armstrong 500 held at Phillip Island. This annual endurance event evolved into Australia's Great Race when it moved to Bathurst three years later. Roxburgh became a Datsun dealer in 1969 and ran the team from his South Melbourne workshop. Teammate Whiteford was a dab hand at circuit racing too, having won the Australian Grand Prix no less than three times, one of them at Bathurst.

For the 1968 Bathurst race, the pair led a trio of Datsun 1600s to a dominating first-second-third finish in Class B. To show how good the newly released 1600s were, they missed fourth place but also finished fifth to eighth in class. Twelve months later Datsun 1600s finished one-two-three-four-five in class with Bruce Stewart/George Garth leading home Roxburgh/Whiteford and Don Smith/Peter Wilson.

The Datsun Racing Team's domination of the small car classes at Bathurst continued in 1970 with two class victories – Class A, Barry Tapsall/Jon Leighton (Datsun 1200) plus Smith and Whiteford who had solo drives to take first and second in Class B with 1600s.

In 1971, pickings were a little slim at Bathurst with only Bruce Stewart picking up a Class B win in a 1600. Twelve months later the Datsun Racing Team had a similar result with a first and third in Class A for Bill Evans and Jon Leighton in 1200 sedans.

For 1973 the Team retired their trusty 1200 sedans and replaced them with a single 1200 coupe. The two-door was a lot quicker with its dual port cylinder head and 5-speed gearbox. With steady development over the next three years the coupe reduced the Class A qualifying time at Bathurst from 3:20 to 2:58, a substantial saving. For 1973, new lead driver Evans teamed up with James Laing-Peach and scored a class win.

With the recent replacement of the 1600 by the 180B, Roxburgh/Whiteford tried hard in the newcomer but could only manage 4th in Class B.

The Team tried a new car and class in 1974 by entering a 240K in Class C (2-3litre cars). Whiteford and team newcomer Stewart McLeod nearly snatched a surprise win against more powerful opposition. When sudden rain fell late in the race Team Manager Roxburgh played an ace by fitting the 240K with quality wet weather tyres. But despite an inspiring drive by Whiteford, the team had to settle for second. In Class A, Evans/Laing-Peach scored a rare DNF.

By 1975 the faithful 1200 had nearly reached its use-by date and the plan was to run a new car, a two-door 120Y sedan, plus the well-sorted 1200 coupe. Both cars were entered for Bathurst and the Sandown lead up event. Unfortunately, the 120Y was less developed than the 1200 plus it was heavier and higher, so proved to be a lot slower than its predecessor.

For both races, the Team switched crews with lead

Roger trying hard in the disappointing 120Y at Sandown in 1975.

drivers Evans/Stewart in the 1200 coupe and Leighton/Bonhomme desperately trying everything to make the 120Y competitive. "I drove Sandown but Jon and I just couldn't qualify the thing for Bathurst, despite some imaginative front suspension settings by Roxburgh."

At Bathurst the lap time difference between the two 1200cc Datsuns was over 10 seconds and because the classes were generally oversubscribed, all cars had to lap within a certain percentage of the fastest in class. Bill was the quickest and we were the slowest. It was the absolute low point of my motor sporting career – a works drive at Bathurst but "Did Not Qualify"!

The final result was a class win for the dominant Evans/Stewart 1200 coupe.

For 1976, the final appearance for the original series of cars at Bathurst, Class A went, yet again, to the Datsun 1200 coupe of Evans/Stewart, driving for John Roxburgh Motors.

For 10 years Datsun Racing Team and Roxburgh Motors concentrated on the Bathurst 500 (miles) and 1000 (kilometres) events but also competed in a variety of lesser touring car events including Sandown (the lead up to Bathurst), Phillip Island and Adelaide International Raceway.

[Nissan took four years away from circuit racing while it concentrated its motorsport resources on rallying but having satisfied that urge it would re-emerge on the racing scene in 1981, rally team re-assigned, to take on the heavy metal goliaths with one of the Datsun 1600's successors.]

Preface

The writing of this story has been an engrossing process to say the least. When I began the project I felt I remembered so little and then I discovered that many of the memories I *did* have, turned out to be fabrications as my brain had apparently laboured to abbreviate and simplify information into file-size chunks, often combining multiple bits into single events and deleting other important chunks. This process also occurs under the influence of one's ego so that, what's stored away will likely tend to enhance, rather than degrade, one's reputation.

The re-remembering of this story, of the what, the who, the when, the where and the how – one that I now feel reasonably confident in presenting as an accurate record, has been an arduous process. It has involved the reading of the race reports from the relevant Australian Motor Racing Yearbooks and many magazines from the time; the watching of all the available YouTube videos of the races we attended; the detailed examination of hundreds of photographs; the discussion with team mates and involved people about the information I'd collected, and then the resolving of conflicting memories and stories, thereby forcing the story to fit together and to fit the evidence.

There have been stories of the Nissan racing team published in recent years which include assertions from various team members and I'm very aware that this book contradicts some of the particulars contained in those narratives. I have to accept that the sources of those stories also suffered from those same memory tricks I've described above, but of course there's also the issue of perspective. This has been written from the standpoint of the team that built, developed, maintained, repaired, pit crewed and yes, loved these cars. It is not unexpected that a driver or a team manager, for example, might see things in a different light. Sadly, said team manager has not survived to counter any disagreeable opinions but if anyone else wishes to dispute the narrative, I'd be happy to enter into discussions.

The STORY – 1981

Following on from Book One... regarding the Akademos Rally, Portman cruised to a fairly easy victory, two minutes plus ahead of Fury/Suffern. Fury had been given the second car for the event over Dunkerton/Beaumont who'd been left out in the cold. Wayne Bell/Col Parry in the Commodore were third nearly ten minutes back and Chris and Simon Brown fourth, a further one minute down in their 180B SSS. This result gave Portman a huge and unassailable lead in the Australian Rally Championship with just the Alpine Rally to go.

Before that though we had one other event to attend. Apart from rally car preparation, much of 1981 was spent in our Braeside workshop building a race car from a standard, P910 Bluebird Turbo which was in Australia for evaluation as a possible addition to the model range available for purchase here.

Fury's last dusty run in the works Stanza which was looking a little the worse for wear at this stage in the 1981 Alpine Rally in late November.

At the Castrol International Rally held around Canberra in March, we ran our Stanza race suspension setup to great effect for the bitumen stages. Then in May the car was damaged in an incident during a Sports Sedan race at Amaroo Park and had to miss the Akademos Rally, the penultimate Australian championship round.

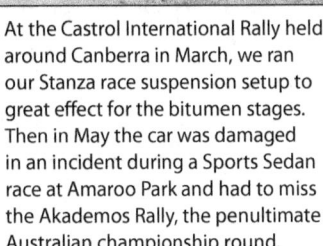

By December it had been repaired and spruced up for this media/practice day at Sandown where George demonstrated he'd successfully made the transition from forest racer to circuit racer.

Fury's rally Stanza did double duty in '81 as it was also being used in the occasional sports sedan race as George was groomed for rebirth as a racing driver. The Stanza missed two ARC rounds due to damage from one race at Amaroo Park in early June.

As we were preparing the Bluebird, a sister car[1] was undergoing similar preparations in Oppama[2], Japan. This car had been assembled incorporating many components we'd made in Australia and sent over for inclusion, including a full bolt-together roll cage. When nearly complete it was air freighted to Australia and arrived at Braeside sometime shortly after the Akademos Rally and was followed soon after by a small team of Japanese mechanics, all of whom we knew from rallying days. What followed was a huge learning curve as our Datsun Rally Team was cast into the furnace and emerged as Nissan Sport Race Team.

The P910 Bluebird had been selected from several possibilities and was a deserving successor to the much exulted P510 (Datsun 1600) and P710 (Violet) with which we'd rallied with much success in Australia. The P910 Bluebird was also assembled locally – although in non-turbo, live rear axle form whereas we were using the turbo boosted, independent rear end model, fully built and sold in Japan.

Looking back, 1981 can be seen as Nissan's transition year between earlier small car class success in Touring Car racing in Australia and what turned into three very exciting years of striving for outright supremacy. Looking at the competition in the 4/5-cylinder class[3], the powers that be must have considered we had some sort of chance of a class win and had we left our ambitions there, we'd no doubt have had considerable success. As it turned out though, the Japanese heroes, Masahiro Hasemi and Kazuyoshi Hoshino opened our eyes to the car's potential to do far better and it was the striving for outright success I think, that makes this a story worthy of a book.

Many standard components proved to be unfit for the task we were demanding of them and this led to a rather high rate of non-finishing, particularly in our first 12 months or so.

---

1 We've become used to referring to this car as BB1 and the first car we prepared in Australia as BB2. Where appropriate I alternatively refer to the cars by their door numbers at the time.
2 The location of Nissan's competition vehicle building factory in Japan.
3 With the FIA (Federation International Automobiles) turbocharged equivalency ratio of 1.4:1 our 1770cc became 2478cc although confusingly, classes published by the ARDC for the James Hardie 1000 in '81 were based on no. of cylinders.

None of us can remember too much about the initial build of BB2 other than what's prompted by a few photos – Peter Anderson and myself, posing for a promo shot, dismantling the standard road car at Braeside, then one of #55 on the apron outside the workshop ready to load up for its first testing session at Calder Raceway and a shot of the two Bluebirds side-by-side in our workshop. There is also a pic of George stepping out of the car in pit lane at Calder with everyone looking rather serious. I'm guessing we were all a bit underwhelmed, maybe beginning the struggle with chronic understeer – which George would not have been enjoying.

Howard Marsden was there with a journo in tow, Fred Gibson is shown leaning against HM's Skyline in the background, thinking what I wonder… I remember that George gave Fred credit for helping him make the transition to circuit racing but we the unwashed, from early days, didn't have a great deal of respect. From about day two George Fury was always much quicker than Fred and we thought the team could have done better. It didn't help that Howard and wife Christine, were besties with Fred and his Christine.

First testing with BB2 at Calder. From left: Fred (hidden by boot lid), George S., George F., Derek and Pete.

At about this time we gained another team member. Ex Moffat fabricator panel beater Dennis Watson joined us, taking charge of wheels and tyres, body repair, painting, and also later as driver of our transporter! It was terrific to suddenly have all of those skills in-house.

Although the Japanese had wanted to delay the Bluebird's debut until 1982,

Sister '81 Bluebird race cars together at last at Braeside.

Howard Marsden was determined that our first race would be the Castrol 400 at Sandown Park[4] but as our race engines hadn't arrived from Japan this wasn't possible. Disappointing though, as we missed an opportunity to iron out some problems that would arise on the much larger stage at Bathurst. On reflection, maybe we should have pushed to do Sandown with the standard engines – we may still have been competitive in the class – well almost – but in any event there really wasn't time and we'd been lucky to get some standard engine laps in at Calder.

Final preparations were a joint effort by Australian and Japanese crews. There were some late nights and a considerable scramble to get the two cars together, everything packed up and off to Mt Panorama but we apparently got it done as, in a photo taken on the way up the Newell Highway by Simon Brown, BB1 (with door #56) is on a trailer behind our 3-litre Urvan being driven by Simon's brother Chris. Also in that photo is a Hertz rent-a-truck, carrying our tyres and baggage, leaning into the left turn at Grong Grong. It was being driven by Dave Thompson, an early part-time team fabricator and a good circuit racer himself, with Les Collins aboard as jockey. Behind car #56 was a second E20 van and trailer carrying car #55 and providing a platform for our on-board cameraman at large.

Thommo setting the pace up the Newell Hwy.

Simon Brown says, *"On the way we, well Les Collins mostly, had to change a sump gasket on one of the Urvans at Numurkah – didn't we ring you for advice?"*.

"Another small memory too was that, on the way, we discovered that the trailers were unregistered! Thanks Howard."

Teammate George Smith (who has contributed hugely to the research for this book) says:

"Our first race was Bathurst '81 with not a lot of testing prior. Just getting two cars to the grid was an accomplishment in itself. I remember one of the recurring driver comments though was, "Too much understeer, I mean plough understeer – I have to back off the throttle or run off the road".

(See the story on the Bluebird's suspension development, page 158).

---

4   The traditional leadup to the main event each year at Bathurst

JAMES HARDIE 1000 MT PANORAMA, BATHURST

1981 was the debut of the 'James Hardie 1000' race after the giant Hardie Group bought out the British Ferodo company and the 'Hardie Ferodo' name was consigned to history.

This race was also the debut of two of the cars that would prove to be our arch rivals in the following three years – Allan Moffat's Peter Stuyvesant sponsored Mazda RX-7 and the black JPS BMW 635, this year driven by Allan Grice who seemed appropriately at home in a black car.

There was also, of course, hoards of V8 engined Commodores, Falcons, Camaros and even a V12 XJS Jaguar, most notably Peter Brock in his red and white Marlboro Holden Dealer Team VC Commodore and Dick Johnson in the blue Palmer Tube Mills XD Falcon[5]. Back then the companies willing to tip in the most money for car racing were the cigarette companies and the television networks – how things have changed!

Classes for the 1981 race were based on the number of cylinders, ie. 4 or 5, 6 plus rotary, and 8+, but this arrangement was unpopular with entrants and CAMS[6] eventually stepped in and insisted that the regular Touring Car classes based on engine capacity be also included, typically adding confusion to the disquiet.

Some humorous episodes from our Bathurst adventures have been remembered by team members and I'll kick off the story with a couple that have escaped the censors to show you, dear reader, that it wasn't all burning of midnight oil and fingers. Dave Thompson remembered the drive to Bathurst in '81:

"I drove the rent-a truck up with all the spares and Les Collins was my jockey. He hadn't been to Bathurst before so I asked Howard, when we arrived at the circuit, if we could drive around it in the truck – he agreed if I'd promise to be careful.

Back in the pits we opened the back doors to the truck to unload and I think it was George and Dennis or maybe the whole crew started giving me grief about the state of the cargo, knowing Howard

---

5   Famous for having crashed out in the 1980 race when the Tru Blue Falcon hit a large rock that had allegedly been rolled onto the track by a drunken spectator at the top of the mountain. The Falcon had been restored to full health with the aid of many fans' donations.

6   The Confederation of Australian motorsport, the then governing body of Motorsport in Australia. Now known as Motorsport Australia.

was close by, Howard nearly soiled his pants with anxiety trying to get across to look in the truck. Just an oxy bottle had a 3 degree lean on it where it hadn't been tied in properly, George did enjoy stirring Howard up."

That first Bathurst 1000 is rather a blur in my mind but I've been reminded that our accommodation that first year was the dorms at Bathurst University!

Thommo also remembered:

"We were all having dinner at The Stagecoach Restaurant in the middle of Bathurst. We the workers were on one table and Howard and the drivers etc. on another. If my memory serves me correctly George S was the ringleader but we all joined in and ordered from the top end of the menu. I have a vague recollection of oysters arriving at the table and the look on Howard's face as they were delivered was PRICELESS!"

Examination of the photos from the first years led to confusion as the first shots of the Bluebirds at Bathurst showed them with black door numbers on a white panel and yet photos from the 1981 start grid and the race showed black panels with white numbers. Was I mixing up 1981 and 1982 photos? Then Den suddenly remembered:

▲ What you could have for $500 extra ▼ Not OK

"I can remember the car numbers being rejected at Bathurst. It was the timekeepers/lap counters who complained they couldn't read them – but for 500 bucks they could pay better attention."

If a team wanted to run something other than white numbers on a black panel they could pay $500 and be allowed to run whatever they wanted, including several coloured sponsor logos incorporating a number[7], and of course Moffat's maroon on white! I can now vaguely remember Howard being disgusted and unwilling to pay this outrageous impost and he had someone summon a sign-writer to fix the doors (the bonnet number remained unchanged). Better to support local small

---

7 Channel 7, 9 and 10 for instance, each of which became door numbers

THE STORY – 1981

The new Nissan team for the 1981 JH1000 at Mt Panorama getting some practice. On the off side, George Smith Fr. and Jamie Drummond Rr, near side, Pete Anderson Fr. and Derek Rawson Rr.

business than further stuff the pockets of the ARDC[8] administrators, would, I believe, have summarised his thoughts on the matter.

On Friday morning Masahiro Hasemi in the Japanese Bluebird Turbo, blitzed the 4/5 cyl class in qualifying with a 2:32.8 lap (which also bettered most of the 6 cylinder/rotary class runners), good enough for 31st place on the grid of 59 cars. Fred Gibson, in BB2 did somewhat less well, earning 43rd grid position and fourth in class. Well, at least we'd given notice Nissan had arrived on the scene.

Good to see our efforts were appreciated.

The final practice on the Friday was on a dry track and, for the front-runners, was mostly about recording a lap time that would get them into the top-ten-shootout[9] on the Saturday.

Despite Saturday morning's heavy rain and high winds the big Chev Camaro driven by Kevin Bartlett managed a quite incredible 2:36.40 to easily win pole position for the race start. Second fastest, a full two seconds slower was the Falcon of Dick Johnson which just pipped Peter Brock's Commodore by two tenths which in turn just

---

8   Australian Racing Drivers' Club, organisers of the James Hardie 1000 event.
9   Known as Hardies Heroes this was a live telecast session from Bathurst where each of the fastest ten cars in practice/qualifying, individually did a lap timed to one hundredth of a second to determine the starting order of the top ten for the race.

bettered the Commodore of Bob Morris, three tenths further back.

The big surprise was that the Mazda RX-7 of Allan Moffat had made it into the shoot-out – the only non V8 in the top ten – and surprise turned to shock when he put the little sports car into fifth place on row three with many heavy metal V8s behind him to out-drag to the first corner on the Sunday.

A suitably bedecked team posing on Sunday morning.

Minutes before the start – all hands on deck.

There was drama for us before the race start though when Dave Thompson, who was holding the drivers' names board in front of Bluebird #56 out on the grid, noticed oil running out from underneath and raised the alarm. One of the Japanese engineers ran out and quickly diagnosed a leaking dry sump oil pump. Japanese engine man Heichan Kato, became the first hero of race day when he managed to change the oil pump out on the grid, just in time for the start at 10.00am.

Both Bluebirds got away satisfactorily and Hasemi/Hoshino led their class until early in the afternoon. Fred Gibson in Car #55 was initially doing OK but at 30 laps became our first casualty, dropping out with a failed suspension rose joint. George Fury didn't get to have a drive.

Just after #56's first pitstop and driver change, Hoshino stopped on the inside of the track just after Hell Corner (turn 1) with a flat battery. He ran back to our pit and although out of breath and in Japlish, managed to get the message across. Dennis grabbed a replacement battery and he and Wyn ran up pit straight to the car, made the swap on the infield grass, and got #56 going again. Sadly, 30 minutes later the car was retired with gearbox failure on lap 66 of the 120 laps finally completed by the eventual winner, Dick Johnson's Ford Falcon.

THE STORY – 1981

Masahiro Hasemi coming down off the mountain.

The story at the front of the race though, was that it began with a frenetic and close battle between Kevin Bartlett in the Channel 9 sponsored Z28 Chev Camaro, Peter Brock in the Holden Dealer Team VC Commodore and Dick Johnson in his Tru Blu XD Falcon and then, after just a few laps, Bob Morris made up the gap to the leaders in his Seiko sponsored Falcon, making it a 4-way battle at the front.

Commodore drivers Garry Rogers and John Harvey were just a few seconds adrift. It was a classic skirmish between the V8s and featured the big names of Touring Car racing in Australia at the time, firing up the fans' passionate love of this class of motorsport.

Brock was the first to stumble just as he was starting to draw away from the others. He and Bartlett had banged door handles going up the mountain and, under brakes at the bottom of Conrod Straight, the Commodore's diff failed giving their team a time consuming job to replace it.

The pace of the remaining leaders continued unabated for 100 laps or so until the race was prematurely and dramatically ended on lap 121. Bob Morris, running in second place, had a coming together with Christine Gibson's Falcon (running in sixth place, albeit six laps down) causing a huge pile up at McPhillamy Park on top of the mountain. Several following cars ploughed in, blocking the track.

More than 60 per cent of the race had been completed so it was declared done according to the regulations and Dick Johnson, the leader at the end of lap 120, the winner. Bob Morris who'd raced Johnson hard all the way placed 2nd even though his Falcon was sitting in a smouldering heap of cars up at McPhillamy Park Corner.

Oh well, at least our Bluebirds survived the race bodily unscathed – we were under way and we'd learned heaps.

1981 AUSTRALIAN ENDURANCE CHAMPIONSHIP

Round 4 The International Resort 300, Surfers Paradise Raceway, 1 Nov.

We'd never had a rally in such a glamorous locale so it was exciting to be on the Gold Coast for our second trip away with the Bluebird.

Johnson, who was one of Queensland's famous sons back in the day, gave the locals raptures when he put his Falcon on pole completing a 3.219km lap in a time of 1:15.3, continuing his dominance of Touring Car racing that year. Brock recorded a 1:15.7 late in practice to win second grid spot and Moffat, who'd done a 1:16.6 earlier in the day, would start on the outside of the front row in third.

Next with a 1:18.0 was Terry Shiel in his RX-7 then Allan Grice in a Commodore with 1:18.2 followed by a disappointed John Goss in the Jaguar XJS with 1:18.4. In seventh place was Alan Browne in the ReCar Commodore with a 1:18.9, and in eighth place Peter McLeod in another RX-7 with a 1.19.1. Phil Alexander, RX-7, Peter Williamson, Toyota Celica, and Neil Cunningham, Commodore, all did 1:20.0 for ninth through twelfth then Graeme Bailey's Celica was 13th with 1:20.2 followed by George Fury in the Bluebird with 1:20.3.

Unfortunately, the Bluebird broke a rear stub axle late in practice and George went off into a ditch – mercifully managing to keep the car upright on its remaining three wheels. We either had no spare to replace it or it was decided the car was too dangerous to race with this fragility and it was withdrawn from the race. George did not start on Sunday and maybe it was just as well.

This was the last Touring Car race for the year and it was a dramatic and exciting one so I've included the details to help set the scene for the following year.

On a dry track but with rain threatening, Dick Johnson, Peter Brock and Allan Moffat started from the front row of the grid and they thundered down the straight to the fastest corner in the country, underneath the Dunlop Bridge. Brock just managed to scrape past into the lead as the track narrowed for turn 2.

Peter Williamson in his Toyota Celica began the 95-lap race leading the Endurance Championship for Drivers (due to his domination of the 2-litre class and the scoring system that awarded equal points for both class and outright positions). He was hoping to wrap it up in the final round.

Light rain began to fall on lap 3 and mayhem began under Dunlop Bridge. First to come unstuck was Alan Brown's Re-Car Commodore, which crashed heavily. Then, at about the 45-minute mark, Peter McLeod lost control of his RX-7 and made huge impact with the tyre wall followed by a multiple end-for-end crash which totally destroyed the car. This was then immediately followed by Peter Williamson wrecking his AEC title chances, to say nothing of his car, with a multiple rollover after impact with the same barrier.

At Brock's fuel and tyre stop the Commodore would not restart and his crew had to push start it, incurring a one-minute penalty.

Then, as if this was not enough carnage for one race, with about 10 laps to go, race leader Johnson had a deflating LHR tyre at the worst place on any circuit in Australia – going under Dunlop Bridge on a slippery surface – and he too went off the track backwards into a gully and rolled heavily. Brock inherited the lead and finished first ahead of Moffat then Grice in the BMW. After the one-minute penalty was applied, Brock was shuffled back to second place and Moffat awarded the win.

Johnson finished his racing year on his roof at Surfers.

Winner of the Australian Endurance Championship for Manufacturers for 1981 was Toyota with 36 points (attained by Graeme Bailey) followed by Ford with 27, then Holden, Mazda and Mitsubishi equal third with 24 points.

Our final event for 1981 was The Alpine Rally in Victoria, held November 21-22. Once again this classic 2-day, 3-division event attracted an over subscribed, sell-out entry, despite the

Geoff Portman & Ross Runnalls ensuring a fit and proper finale.

already won Championship. The LCCA[10] organised an exceptional event that was graced with fine and sunny weather. The maximum 80 cars were flagged away on the Bright Speedway and on into the magnificent surrounding pine plantations on a beautiful Saturday morning.

Fury and Suffern led the event until around half way, when an off on a night bitumen section allowed Geoff Portman and Ross Runnalls through to win quite easily in the end on 5:58:12, just over nine minutes to the good of Fury/Suffern on 6:07:14, who were nearly seven minutes ahead of a third Stanza, that of Doug Thompson/Ron Lugg.

So ended that golden period of rallying in Australia. We were the last of the manufacturers in Australia to withdraw from the sport and together with the demise of the Castrol International and the Southern Cross International rallies it seemed like a line had been drawn. We were free to concentrate on the next challenge.

A not quite politically correct cartoon on the release of the Bluebird Racing 'Limousine' from John Stoneham.

---

10 The Light Car Club of Australia, now defunct

1982

In the reasonably short break from race meetings over the Christmas period we worked hard to rectify some of the cars' shortcomings that had already become evident.

George Smith recounts:

"Apart from the turbocharger, which was to haunt us nearly through to the end of the Bluebird program, we chased failures right down the drive train: gearbox, tail shaft, drive shafts, inner and outer CV joints. We sourced and built replacements until everything under the car could be relied upon."

See further info in the section on development, from page 165

Barry Bray joined us! A printer by trade but also a naturally talented machinist and fabricator. We'd been consulting with him for a couple of years and, when the opportunity arose, he left his job in Adelaide, moved to Melbourne and became part of the team. He would play an important part in the cars' development and success over the ensuing three years.

We'd been particularly troubled by rear wheel flange failures – the flange breaking off the short stub axle held in the trailing arm, which obviously and dramatically caused a wheel to part company with the car. Attempts to resolve this included having axles made from higher-grade steel and then by upping the flange thickness. When these continued to break despite our best efforts, this became one of Bazza's first projects. He designed, engineered and welded into the A arms, a floating hub solution that proved to be the final fix.

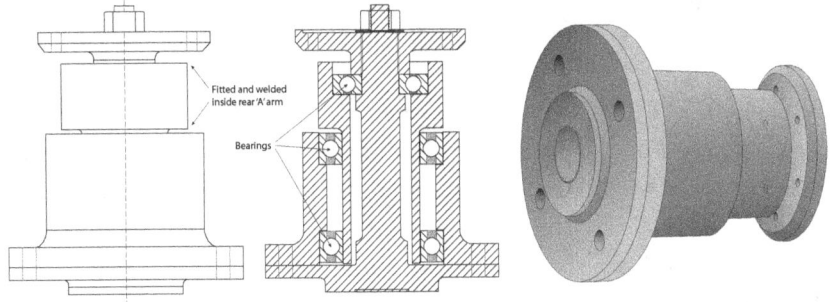

Sometime around February, Howard came to Braeside one morning and announced we'd be moving operations to a newly built factory duplex in Healey Road, South Dandenong (about 700 metres from Nissan's Head Office)! Well, that was certainly welcome news and you could just about see George S. licking his lips. Unfortunately for us though, George accepted a short-term contract in the USA and he immediately took a three-month furlough to join a Can-Am team over there.

Two Bluebird racers at our new workshop shortly after the mezzanine was built. (Jamie's 120Y there in the background.)

By the time he returned around June, we'd prepped and moved into our new Healey Road home. I remember us there knocking a double door sized hole in the wall adjoining the mirror-image west-side factory and a carpenter was organised to build saloon doors. We spent another three weekends grinding smooth and acid etching the concrete floors and next time we visited we discovered our brand new steel workbenches all rusted!

Another couple of visits were spent applying coats of clear two-pack to the floors and soon after that we had a very large steel mezzanine built in the east-side factory for parts and tyres storage. This mezzanine-building job was given to the Nissan Purchasing Manager's brother and was apparently put up without a permit. A building inspector arrived at the workshop one day and Howard had to come and 'speak' to him and help him load a set of wheels into his car. We still had to make modifications to the ceiling height on the back half of it but at least it wasn't torn down.

Also explained to us at around this time was that Fred Gibson would be running one of the cars from his Sydney 'Road and Track' workshop with his own mechanics – our resources and efforts would be split for the first half of '82 with Gibson to compete in the AMSCAR series at Amaroo Park, Sydney. Fury would run the Australian Touring Car Championship (ATCC) from Melbourne and we'd join up again for the Australian Endurance Championship (AEC) in the second half of the year.

As it turned out the Melbourne team did only the local rounds of the ATCC – Sandown, Calder and Adelaide in '82, but also the final AMSCAR series round in Sydney. Fred Gibson ran the full AMSCAR series but also the first ATCC round at Sandown and placed seventh in the aggregate score for the two heats that make up that round. Fury placed second outright at our home track of Calder! A gearbox failure

DNF at the Adelaide round may have indicated we'd had a whiff of success and were pushing the boost too high. We made some serious progress though.

Touring Car racing classes for 1982 were basically, up to and including 3000cc and 3000–6000cc. With a forced induction equivalency ratio of 1.4:1 our 1770cc engined cars became 2,478cc so we were well inside the <3000cc class. I think it was only the most optimistic of us at the time who thought us capable of much more than class wins that year but it wasn't far into the event calendar that we all began seeing our cars as capable of mixing it with the V8 heroes of the day.

1982 AMSCAR Better Brakes series, Amaroo Park

Prior to 1982 the AMSCAR series had been specifically for up to 3-litre touring cars but this year the promoters[1] announced it would henceforth be for outright contenders. Probably because full live TV broadcast had been promised and the series had a large following.

For 1982 this series consisted of four rounds and each consisted of a preliminary ten lapper and then a 25-lap race totalling 48.5 kms. Although the Touring Car Championship rounds and the AMSCAR Series events were somewhat interleaved in the first half of each year, I've decided to cover these series separately here so as not to detract from the interest in each. And as the ATCC was by far the more interesting, I'll get the AMSCAR rounds out of the way first.

As Amaroo was Fred Gibson's home track, he would be the Nissan flag bearer for the time being.

AMSCAR Round 1, March 14

The preliminary race, on a dry track, saw a flag to flag domination from pole position by Peter Brock, followed by the two Amaroo specialists, Terry Shiel and Barry Jones, both in RX-7 Mazdas. The main race was the last race of the day and run in heavy rain. Brock dominated once again although it was an exciting race for fans with the two RX-7s, Colin Bond, in the Bartlett Camaro, Dick Johnson's Falcon, Commodores of Allan

---

1   The Australian Racing Drivers' Club

Grice and Clive Benson-Browne, the Falcon of Garry Wilmington etc., slipping and sliding and racing hard, swapping positions. Fred Gibson in car #56 started seventh on the grid and worked his way backward to finish 14th, more than a lap adrift. On the TV coverage he was seen only once after the start – when Brock lapped him.

AMSCAR Round 2, April 11

The second AMSCAR round was run in much improved weather and was again a competitive affair with most of the big guns, this time including John Goss in a V12 Jaguar. Brock's Commodore was strangely down on power and seemed to have had a role reversal with Allan Grice's similar car, which was this time fastest and started from pole. Gibson was again disappointing and could not better 18th on the grid. In this race he was able to improve somewhat and finished 7th, at least on the same lap as the winner, Allan Grice.

Reproduced from the 1982 Australian Motor Racing Yearbook
Seventh in Rnd 2 – Fred's best in the AMSCAR series in '82.

AMSCAR Round 3, May 23

For the third AMSCAR round Moffat decided to turn up and claim some of the TV limelight for Peter Stuyvesant with his blue and white RX-7. He dominated the weekend, winning both his heat and the main event.

At this round they ran separate heats for the V8s and the rotaries plus 3-litre cars, which were expected to be the slower. Ironically, half of these were actually faster than the V8s. Gibson managed eighth place on the grid and slipped only slightly in the race to finish ninth.

Positions at race's end were Moffat and Shiel in RX-7s, Bond's Camaro, Grice's Commodore, then a Falcon, two more Commodores, another RX-7, then the #56 Bluebird, which was again almost not seen in the TV coverage. This weekend was notable for being the first time the RX-7s dominated the V8s at Amaroo, a circuit that was also supposed to suit the heavy metal. The writing was definitely on the wall.

AMSCAR Round 4, July 11

Fury joined the fun for Rnd 4 and we ran both #55 and #56. After threatening for the series, Terry Shiel lived up to promise and put his

Eurocars RX-7 Mazda on pole with a 53.4 second lap.

Grice was next fastest qualifier with 53.7, followed by 'Big Revs Kev' Bartlett with 54.0. Richards (BMW) and Gibson in #56 were next on the grid, both on 54.7. George was a way back in ninth position with a 55.0.

In the race, Shiel led from go to whoa, setting a new touring car lap record in the process, although clearly the RX-7 was no touring car. Grice's second place in the Re-Car Commodore was enough to wrap up the AMSCAR title for 1982 and Bartlett placed third.

George got squeezed between two Falcons, got a touch and spun across the track missing everyone, then slid past the end of the Armco and disappeared down into a gully. One commentator quipped that George'll need a navigator and a Halda to find his way back to the track. He did though and set too to make up lost ground. Gibson seemed to be fairing better, battling with Richards' BMW but then spun. Fury finished 10th and Gibson 12th.

1982 AUSTRALIAN TOURING CAR CHAMPIONSHIP

For 1982 CAMS had decided to specify and enforce minimum weights for each make and model. This together with Brock's decision to use the big-valved cylinder heads, from the Marlboro Holden Dealer Team 'Brock Special' Commodores in his lighter VH Commodore race car. The ensuing ruckus over that, together with the advances Moffat had made in the performance of his RX-7, would be the defining factors in this season's ATCC Series.

A somewhat vicious dispute between CAMS and the MHDT[2] regarding the eligibility of the high performance cylinder heads raged throughout most of the season. In the subsequent settlement, Brock was disqualified from all rounds of this championship from Calder onwards, strangely though with the exception of the second round at Symmons Plains.

Championship points were awarded on a 9–6–4–3–2–1 basis to the first six place-getters in each class at each round. Bonus points were awarded on a 4–3–2–1 basis to the first four place-getters, irrespective of class, at each round. Results from seven of the eight rounds could be retained by each driver.

---

2 Confederation of Australian Motorsport and the Marlboro Holden Dealer Team

ATCC Round 1 Sandown International Raceway, Victoria, February 17-18

A very hot weekend saw many cars suffering heat related issues, including the big Camaro boiling its brake fluid, and the organisers being very embarrassed when the scales they'd brought along to enforce the new weight limits were affected and gave wildly varying readings leading to the abandonment of their weighing efforts.

In qualifying, Fury did a 1:17.5 to put #55 in 13th place on the grid, easily the fastest of the up to three-litre class. Gibson's 1:19.2 in #56 (16th on grid) was third fastest in class after Steve Masterton's V6 Capri with a 1:18.1.

For the second practice session the boost pressure was raised on both Nissans and each proceeded to destroy its turbocharger, hopefully prompting more caution with that wastegate screw. In the outright category, Johnson managed a 1:12.9, Brock a 1:13.0 and Moffat a 1:14.4.

Our first meeting in 1982. Notice the size of the exhaust outlet compared to later shots (see better pics page 182) and how small the original 15" wheels look.

This round was run in two, 16-lap heats and in the first, Fury finished tenth, on the same lap as winner, Dick Johnson in his Falcon, and more than a lap ahead of Masterton in second place in their class. Gibson placed 12th, more than a lap down. In Heat 2, Gibson placed 11th and Fury retired with an overheating engine near the finish. Combined results for the two races were Johnson with two heat wins obviously the winner, Brock claimed second with his second and third placings and then Bartlett. Gibson was classified as overall 9th and Fury 11th.

Video of the second heat shows: Johnson just managed to lead into turn 1 followed by Bartlett in the Camaro then Moffat followed by Brock then Cullen. The race settled down with Brock getting past Moffat and then harrying Bartlett but not able to pass. From half way, Johnson led Bartlett then Brock, Moffat, Murray Carter (Falcon), Jansen and Brown (Commodores), Wilmington (Falcon), Harrington (Commodore) and Fury, half a lap adrift. Gibson was further back and was lapped by the leaders at about ¾ distance. Fury retired just two laps from the finish.

At least one of the Nissans was beginning to show its potential.

ATCC Round 2 Calder Park Raceway, Victoria, February 27-28

In Saturday's qualifying at our home, and the Bluebird's favourite circuit, George managed a 47.05 to be outright ninth fastest, beating two of the favoured V8s. The big guns qualified with mid-46 second times. It had been decided Gibson and car #56 would remain in Sydney for the rest of the ATCC series and focus instead on the AMSCAR series at Amaroo Park, so George and car #55 had our full attention for the remaining races of this series.

The 50-lap race was a typically tight contest between Johnson, Brock and Bartlett until the Camaro's brake master cylinder failed at about ¼ distance, leaving the arch rivals to battle it out, Brock eventually got the better of it and finished ahead. Fury gradually worked his way forward and at the end of the race was just 28 seconds behind Johnson!

The excitement of the race however was overshadowed by controversy and back biting surrounding the eligibility of the Commodores. It seemed Brock and some of the other Commodore drivers were trying to make conciliatory efforts, arriving at Calder with ballast to make up the extra weight of the MHDT Specials. The old boys at CAMS were having none of it though and would only allow them to race a legitimate MHDT car or a lighter VH with the small valve head. The final results of the Calder race were not known until much later, after the Supreme Court challenge had been heard and the Confederation had handed down its edict. Brock was disqualified and his Calder win overturned.

George was finally awarded second place to Dick Johnson and had comprehensively won the 3-litre class by more than a lap.

From this point we realised we had a car that could mix it with the top contenders and we skipped the next four rounds of the Championship to settle into our new workshops at Dandenong South and to double down on development and iron out some issues. Fred Gibson and his small band failed to excite with their efforts in the AMSCAR series in Sydney.

During this time we managed to begin to unpick the cause of the problems with the front suspension. At Fred's insistence we had incrementally increased the front spring rates to 1400lbs and the anti-roll bar diameter to something approaching the size of a crow bar – just ridiculous for the weight of the car.

On reflection it should have been obvious there was a geometry problem – the front roll centre was shifting as the car leaned into a corner and all the brains-trust was able to come up with at the time was to try and stop the body roll with springs and sway bar, no wonder early action photos of the cars often showed daylight between tyres and road. Once again it was left to the boys in the workshop to get to the bottom of this issue and then come up with a solution. See the section on development of the Bluebird's suspension beginning on page 158.

We were told our developments would be tested at Amaroo and the results fed back to us. I don't remember that happening and anyway, they weren't really going fast enough to meaningfully test anything.

ATCC Round 3 Symmons Plains Raceway, Tasmania, March 6-7

This event was the first of the five ATCC rounds we did not attend in 1982 but, for the record…

In qualifying, Brock was quickest with a 59.70 second lap, Johnson next best with 1:00.4, Bartlett third with 1:01.03 and then Moffat with 1:01.32.

It was another hard fought battle between the V8 heroes of the day with Moffat nibbling at their heels. Brock, running under appeal to his disqualification, won from pole position after Johnson initially got the jump on him from the start. Brock soon prevailed though and led through to the finish. Johnson followed him home in front of Bartlett's Camaro, Cullen's and Parsons' Commodores etc. Moffat's Mazda overheated, due to too much time sitting in the Camaro's slipstream, and blew a rotor seal at half distance while running fourth.

Strangely, after Brock had gained ascendency over Johnson at the previous round at Calder but been subsequently disqualified, for this round his first placing stood, even though he'd turned up at Symmons Plains with the exact same car. There was much head scratching to say nothing of Victorian Supreme Court arguing and the resulting blood letting that took place in 1982.

ATCC Round 4. Oran Park Raceway, NSW – March 20-21

Probably due to the Supreme Court's rather tardy dismissal of Brock's appeal against his disqualification at Calder, there was a dispute over whether he'd be allowed to race at Oran Park. Fortunately for the fans, Brock's finding of a CAMS rule allowing a competitor to race while an appeal was pending, and his lodging of a further appeal, meant that he did front up for practice at Round 4.

On a warm and dry beginning to the weekend Brock was able to do a 1:15.9 lap to claim pole, Johnson a 1:16.7 to also grab a front row position. Barry Jones in his RX-7 just recently upgraded with a Peripheral-Ported[3] 12A motor was quick with a third fastest, 1:17.0. Bartlett's 1:17.4, and Moffat's 1:18.4 placed them next in order.

Race day though was damp and while most teams elected to start the race on slicks[4], Dick Johnson gambled on 'wet' (grooved) tyres which did look the better choice initially. Moffat however was best away and sprinted down to turn 1 in the lead followed by Brock, Bartlett, Jones, Johnson, who'd made an uncharacteristically tardy start.

By lap 5 the rain had abated and a dry line was showing on the track – Johnson's tyre choice no longer looked the goods and he was slipping back. His pitstop soon after was slow and he was no longer in contention.

It must have been an entertaining race to watch as rain showers came and went and there was much tyre swapping, albeit with limited success in out-guessing the weather gods. Peter Brock even had a very rare spin as he battled a wet track on slick tyres!

No one was able to catch him though and the final positions were Brock, Bartlett, Shiel, Jones etc. with Moffat back in eleventh after a difficult race. Brock's win was taken from him later when his eligibility dispute was finally settled, so the record shows a win for Kevin Bartlett.

ATCC Round 5 Lakeside International Raceway, Queensland, April 3-4

Round 5 at Dick Johnson's home circuit proved to be instead a showcase for Allan Moffat's Mazda. Not only was he fastest in practice, earning pole position on the start grid with a 56.8, but he led the race from beginning to end and set a new lap record in the process.

Johnson's 57.3 got him second place on the grid alongside Moffat and Brock's 57.6 and Bartlett's 58.3 saw the two of them on the second row, Brock complaining about a lack of power at high revs. The usual suspects

---

3   Standard Mazda rotary engines have inlet and exhaust ports that pass through the engine's end plates. Considerable performance advantage could be achieved by blocking these and porting instead though the rotor housings.

4   Dry weather race tyres have no tread and are known as 'slicks'.

made up the remaining places in a rather disappointing, 14-car field.

While Moffat made a great start and took control early, Bartlett limped to the pits with a broken axle. Johnson and Brock raced enthusiastically until a rock thrown up by the Falcon, which was using all of the circuit plus some, broke Brock's windshield causing him to put some space between the two of them. The only position swapping was going on further back in the field so it was all a bit dull. Moffat won by a good margin to Johnson then Brock, who was later disqualified once again, leaving the Ron Wanless Re-Car Commodore, the only other car to complete the 35 laps, with third.

ATCC Round 6 Wanneroo Park, Western Australia, April 27-28

A good number of top-level competitors made the trip across the Nullabor for the Wanneroo meeting although Moffat and Fury were not among them. Johnson was first out onto the circuit after a surprise announcement that cars would be weighed on their first exit of the pits. A separate jack needed to be positioned under each wheel so each car weighing was a rather slow and fiddly process. Johnson thereby had the advantage of an empty track with enough time on the circuit by himself to do two flying laps, sufficient for him to capture pole with a 1:2.56. Later, Brock grabbed second place on the grid with 1:2.65 then Grice third in the first RE-Car Commodore (a lighter VC model with small-valve heads) with 1:3.20. The second Re-Car Commodore with Ron Wanless at the wheel took fourth with a 1:4.09.

The race start went as per the script: Johnson, Brock, Grice, Wanless, but behind, Cullen had designs on fourth, tried a kamikaze overtake and got caught up in a melee with the Commodores of Harrington, Parsons and Negus – there were cars spinning off all over. Grice had been pressuring Brock and then, on lap 19 slipped past the red and white Marlboro Holden, which would have been galling for Brock. Then, on lap 23, Grice suddenly found himself leading the race after Johnson coasted into the pits with a dead engine.

And so the race wound down with Brock following Grice then Wanless and Steve Harrington, a very successful weekend for Holden and especially for the Re-Car team after Brock again had his second place taken away, leaving the two yellow and white Commodores in the records with first and second.

ATCC Round 7 Adelaide International Raceway, South Australia, May 1-2

At this very fast track, traditionally suited to the big V8s, it was demoralising to discover that Moffat's Stuyvesant Mazda was now the car everyone was trying to catch. It easily achieved pole position with a 57.7 after just two quick laps. Johnson and Brock were next best with 58.3 and 58.8 respectively. Fury earned sixth on the grid with a time of 59.8 achieved after another turbocharger blow-up.

Always a star performer, Glen Dix gets the cars away in style.

At the start of the 40-lapper, Bartlett launched the Camaro before flamboyant Flag Marshall Glen Dix had dropped the flag and he slipped past Brock and Johnson from the second row. Moffat was already disappearing into the distance, easily first into turn 1 at the end of the long front straight. The Bluebird broke its third gear synchro hub on leaving the grid and it seemed George was going nowhere until he discovered he still had a few gears available and took off in pursuit of the peloton.

He was actually making progress through the field until lap 18 when, having advanced to about tenth, was forced to retire – broken parts in the gearbox having compounded the failure.

Moffat, I think, undid himself due to over-confidence. Leading by a handsome margin on lap 28 and about to lap Wilmington's Falcon, he attempted the pass in a treacherous spot and they came together, the big Falcon coming off decidedly the better. Johnson swept into the lead to the delight of the hoards of Ford fans and was followed closely by Bartlett, albeit carrying a one minute penalty for the jumped start.

At race end it was Dick Johnson first, Bartlett second, Brock third and Allan Browne's Commodore fourth. These positions were shuffled though when firstly Bartlett's penalty was applied and much later Brock was again disqualified. The record for this event shows Johnson, 13 points for first, Bartlett, 9 points for second and Browne, 6 points for third. No points for us.

With George's dismal ATCC points tally it was decided we could better use our time to prepare for the Endurance Championship and we didn't make the journey north to the Gold Coast for the final round.

ATCC Round 8 Surfers Paradise Raceway, Queensland, May 15-16

For the record: Like the Adelaide track, Surfers had been considered a circuit suited to the heavy metal and the V8s were expected to dominate the final ATCC round for the year. Despite this, Moffat again easily qualified fastest, reeling off a 1:14.8 on his first quick lap – 1.4 seconds better than Johnson's lap record there. No one else could get close. Brock's best was 1:15.3 then Johnson, disappointing at his 'other home' circuit with 1:16.1. Grice was next quickest with a 1:16.3, a full second slower than Brock's larger valved Commodore.

This time Moffat didn't get away from the start quite so smartly and he had to follow Johnson and Brock into turn 1 and with Grice hot on his tail. On lap 4 Moffat managed to slip past Brock and the four of them continued to race hard and close until lap 12 when Moffat made his move on Johnson. Once again the Mazda and a Ford had a coming together but surprisingly this time it was Johnson who spun off into the wet grass and biffed the barrier, ending his race.

Moffat continued into the lead and went on his merry way, leaving Brock, Grice and Richards behind but Grice managed to get past Brock before the finish so in the end Moffat won at a cruise by a demoralising 5.1 seconds from Grice and then, following Brock's much later sixth disqualification for the season, Richards went into the records as third.

Dick Johnson was eventually recorded as winner of the Touring Car Championship with 53 points after Brock's appeal against his disqualifications was much later dismissed. But by then, who cared other than Dick and I guess Peter (not quite) Perfect[5]?

Had it not been for the disqualifications, Brocky would have blitzed the field with a total of 72 points to Dick's 53, Moff's 27 and KB's 23.

Quick RX-7s had peripheral porting for 1982 and were now all much faster than the Ford Capris. There were the beginnings of rumblings about whether RX-7s, obviously a sports car, ought be permitted to run

---

5 Peter Perfect was one of Brock's nicknames at the time.

in Touring Car races. These were to continue and if anything, grow ever louder over the following two years, helped in spades by all the other liberties that were both granted to and stolen by the RX-7 racers.

CRC 300, 155 laps of Amaroo Park, NSW August 7-8

This was not a round of the Endurance Championship in 1982. It was well supported by most of the major players however, some of whom used the event to give their second tier drivers some time in the car they'd be sharing in the AEC races over the coming months.

Formula 1 star Allan Jones (driving with Barry Jones) captured pole in BJ's RX-7 and next to him sat Terry Shiel in his. Next was Allan Brown taking the first stint in the Grice Re-Car Commodore, then another RX-7 for Graham Alexander completed row two. Gibson and Fury were fifth and sixth together on row three. Larry Perkins in the 05 Commodore and Richards' BMW were back on the sixth row in 11th and 12th! Video of the event shows our team's two beauties, Margie Fury and Christine Gibson, on lap scoring duty!

Gibson started better than Fury and they were sixth and eleventh exiting the first corner. Gibson was fourth over the line at the end of lap 1. Allan Jones had started best though and 14 laps later, had extended his lead to more than eight seconds over Shiel's RX-7.

Fury was running seventh behind Perkins at about lap 50 and Jones had lapped second place Alexander's RX-7 on lap 63. At half distance Gibson was second and Fury third – neither had yet stopped.

After both Nissans had completed their scheduled stops, it was the Jones' RX-7 with a lap plus about six seconds to Fury, then about 40 seconds to Gibson. Perkins was next then Richards and then Grice who was catching them both. In an interview from the pits, Peter Brock says that the Nissans are, for him, the most impressive cars in the race.

Fury un-lapped himself on about lap 120 and was taking four seconds

Fury is lapping Grice for a second time and is almost completely past going into the corner, obliging Grice to give way. He does not and nudges the rear of #55, inducing a spin into the wall.

a lap from Jones' lead! With ten laps to go George was lapping Grice for a second time and although he was almost completely past, coming onto the main straight Grice did not give way, as was mandated, and hit the rear corner of the Bluebird, spinning George into the pit wall.

So, Jones (B&A) won by a lap and a bit to Fred Gibson, who was two laps up on Grice. It was disappointing, if not galling, to see Fred chummying up to Grice at the trophy presentation.

Den had a big job to repair the car before the first round of the Endurance Championship at Oran Park. He managed to acquire a blue Bluebird (shouldn't they all be that colour?) and had to unpick the RH rear quarter panel and the rear taillight panel from it, the boot lid and several sundry parts were also required. After removing these parts from the racer the boot floor and subframe had to be straightened and once everything was back where it belonged, the blue panels welded on. A not insignificant job was the careful removal of the fuel filler flaps in the boot lid and their fitment into the blue boot lid.

Ouch, that's not going to be easy to fix.

Once all in fresh white 2-pack and sign writing completed, the incident was quickly forgotten and its memory has just recently resurfaced when the current owner of this car was stripping it for restoration and discovered blue paint underneath the rear spoiler. It's incredible how much memory can be rekindled by such a simple discovery.

Other body parts were scavenged from the blue-bird in response to a misadventure at the chicane in Healey Road with one of the TRXs to which we fitted turbo kits but that would be speaking ill of the departed and besides, I'm getting off track, so to speak.

1982 AUSTRALIAN ENDURANCE CHAMPIONSHIP

Classes for this series were: up to 1600cc, 1601-2000cc, 2001-3000cc and 3001-6000cc.

Somewhat similar to Formula 1 these days, the AEC in 1982 had both a Championship for Makes as well as one for Drivers. This was an attempt to keep both camps interested, as well as the viewing public who had previously shown little interest in a competition for car makers.

The #56 Bluebird was back in Melbourne and the Nissan team reunited for the full series.

AEC Round 1 Perrier Gold Cup, Oran Park, NSW – August 22

The 35-car starting grid for the first round had Moffat's Mazda on pole with a qualifying time of 1:16.1, Johnson's new XE Falcon with a 1:16.9, Fury's #55 Bluebird with 1:17.3 (1.5 bar boost), Bartlett's Camaro with 1:17.4, Jones' RX-7 with 1:17.6.

Gibson who'd qualified 11th fastest broke a rear drive shaft at the start and could not continue.

At five laps in, Johnson was being harried by Bond (having a turn in the Camaro) then it was about five seconds to Moffat then a further three seconds to Fury. He was into the pits though with a turbo boost pressure leak on lap 6, resuming eight laps later. Moffat harassed the rear of Johnson's Falcon until the pit stops but slowed and stopped soon after with a broken throttle linkage, leaving Johnson clearly in the lead until he too visited the pits, this time for an unscheduled rear tyre change. Fury was circulating rapidly again and un-lapped himself but was obviously too far back to threaten the podium.

Bob Morris' white Falcon eventually won, Dick Johnson, 25 seconds back in the TruBlu Falcon was second, and McLeod's RX-7 third.

Endurance Championship Drivers' points from Oran Park that related to our efforts were: Parmenter (V6 Capri) 9, Morris (Falcon) 9, Fury (Bluebird) 6, Johnson (Falcon) 6, McLeod (Strongbow RX-7) 4, Barry Seton (V6 Capri) 4. (9-6-4-3-2-1 points awarded for each class)

And for the Manufacturers' title: Ford 9, Nissan 6, Toyota 6, Mazda 4, BMW 3, Holden 2. (9-6-4-3-2-1 points awarded for the highest placed finisher for each marque).

AEC Round 2 The Castrol 400 at Sandown Raceway, Vic., September 11-12

This race, the second most prestigious event on the Australian Motor Sport Calendar after the James Hardie 1000, was conducted on the original (shorter) track with it's atrocious pits and very narrow, and dangerous pit lane. Late in the race these latter factors would contribute to a huge controversy.

The starting grid had Peter Brock (new SS 05 Marlboro Holden Dealer Team Commodore) on pole, with Dick Johnson's TRU BLU XE Falcon alongside him. On the second row were Allan Grice (Re-Car Commodore) and Colin Bond driving Bartlett's dark-blue, Channel 9, Z28 Camaro and on the third row was John Harvey (Dealer Team Commodore #25) and George Fury (Bluebird #55) with Moffat (LHD Stuyvesant RX-7) right behind.

Up the back straight for the first time it was Brock leading Johnson followed by Grice then Bond and then Moffat. Fury was seventh or eighth but Brock soon had gearbox trouble and was forced to retire. In the first segment of the race George was harrying Bondy everywhere but on the two long straights. Gibson was back in the pack tussling with 3-litre class contenders.

Here, Grice narrowly leads Bond then Fury and Moffat.

At 25 laps, Grice led Harvey by 2.3 seconds and Moffat by a further 1.48 seconds. Next was Johnson another 12.5 seconds back, then Rogers eight seconds behind Dick and Morris 13 seconds behind Rogers. Moffat passed Grice to go into lead on lap 33.

On lap 48 it was Grice, 48 seconds ahead of Johnson. There was much activity in the pits and several on-track incidents so cars were dropping out left and right. On lap 52 it was Grice followed by Moffat then Harvey, Rogers, Shiel and O'Brien. Moffat pitted for fuel on lap 47 and noticeably sped down pit lane striking a TV camera on the way! Cables from the camera became tangled under Bob Morris' Falcon which stopped and retired on the back straight, unable to select gears. Mayhem!

Moffat was shown the first of several black flags[6]. He returned to his pit, again at speed, stopped for about three seconds and sped out again. On lap 61 Fury is up to sixth but down a lap. Gibson's scheduled stop of 20 seconds on lap 68 was easily the quickest to that time. Grice's stop took 56 seconds.

Moffat and Gibson were both penalised one minute for excessive speed in the pit lane. At lap 88, in the 3-litre class, Fury led Gibson by one lap and Fred had two laps on third place. On lap 93 Fury again suffered boost loss and pitted – the pressure coupling had come adrift of the turbo's compressor, as it had at Oran Park, three weeks prior.

The final laps were filled with drama and controversy as Moffat was repeatedly black flagged – which he ignored. He finished in first place but Allan Grice was shown the chequered flag, second was awarded to Dick Johnson, then Harvey/Scott. Moffat lodged a protest.

After subsequent hearings Moffat was reinstated as the official winner making he and Mazda the only happy parties. Almost everyone at the circuit that day was scathing in their criticism of the organisers, The Light Car Club of Australia, its officials, CAMS, and of course Allan Moffat but his was the name that now appears in the record as the race winner. The first time a Japanese made car had won the annual Sandown Endurance race.

Fred Gibson was officially eighth, three laps down but a substantial winner in the 3-litre class, eleven laps ahead of second place, the Mazda RX-3 driven by Myhill/Bundy, the only other 3-litre finisher. Fury did not resume after his late race drama with loss of boost pressure.

Endurance Championship Drivers' points relating to our efforts following Sandown's Castrol 400 were Parmenter (V6 Capri) 12, Johnson (Falcon) 10, Moffat 9, Morris (Falcon) 9, Gibson 9, Fury 6, McLeod (Strongbow RX-7) 4. Barry Seton (V6 Capri) 4. (*9-6-4-3-2-1 points awarded for each class)

And for the Manufacturers' title, Nissan 15, Toyota 15, Ford 13, Mazda 13, Holden 8, BMW 3. (*9-6-4-3-2-1 points awarded for the highest placed finisher in each class)

---

6   A black flag together with a car number is shown by an official to a passing car when that car is required to enter the pits and report to a marshall.

AEC Round 3 The James Hardie 1000, Bathurst, NSW – October 1-3

Whereas classes in 1981 were based on the number of cylinders, the 1982 regulations were simplified to Class A – over 3000cc and Class B – under 3000cc but, as a round of the AEC a secondary class structure also applied which included up to 1600cc, 1601–2000cc and 2001–3000cc – more confusion and ARDC nose-thumbing at CAMS.

Memories from the boys – Dave Thompson:

"Surely one of us can put together a story about the nights at the Uni with the Japs and the dried fish stuff they ate, which we decided was the reason it took four of them to lift a gearbox. Also that big Jap guy that drank all the saki that they'd heated in saucepans!"

We couldn't so that will have to do. And then Den Watson:

"I remember when we hooked up with the Jap mechanics in 1982 there was much frivolity and back slapping – "you battery, you battery!!" It was great to be recognised and remembered by them."

Bathurst qualifying electrified us! Both Japanese and Australian Bluebirds qualified to run in Hardies Heroes – Hasemi in Car #56 fifth and Fury in #55, seventh fastest! Turbo 4-cylinder cars in Bathurst's top 10 was a shock to the V8 old boys club but they would have to get used to it as we were just warming up!

Ours were the first turbocharged cars and the first 4-cylinder cars to run in the Saturday morning shoot-out. Masahiro Hasemi was the first ever, and still the only, Japanese driver, and George Fury only the second Australian Rally Champion (after Colin Bond in '79), to compete in the shoot-out (this being the last year each driver got to do two timed laps.)

Two engines to change after qualifying plus a spare.

Both Nissan drivers managed a good lap for Hardies Heroes but Hasemi's first was a great one, 2:18:87, an incredible 14.7 seconds faster than his best in 1981. On his second though, no doubt with the boost screwed up a little further, car #56 suffered a turbocharger

THE STORY – 1982

Breakfast at the Mt Panorama paddock, pop-up restaurant. From left, Cato san, Saito san, your author concentrating on his eggs and bacon, Mr Gun's back, George Smith, and Fred's mechanic, Wyn Ellerie.

Just out of our rented pantec and into the sunlight. Den adding even more shininess.

RaceCam has sure come a long way since 1982. Temporarily during practice, front spoiler mounted and side mounted big clunky cameras all held in place with red race tape. GoPros they were not.

Bathurst pits with everyone getting organised for the start of practice.

Gibson on two wheels coming down off the mountain during qualifying.

A relaxed Hasemi awaits the start of The Great Race from grid position 3.

Half a second into The Great Race, so far so good.

In sixth place Hasemi heads into the pits for their first stop.

failure up on top of the mountain and it limped back to the pits trailing blue smoke. He'd been the fastest in every sector to that point. Not to worry, with his first lap Hasemi had been able to able to improve his grid position from fifth to third for Sunday's race. Fury's best of 2:20:613 in the shoot-out saw him slip a couple of places, from seventh to tenth.

We all worked hard that night but went to bed happy and awoke excited.

On the grid there were a somewhat embarrassing, 31 cars between Fury's #55 Bluebird and the first Capri, the next under 3-litre car!

George made a great start and was up alongside Hasemi as they approached Hell corner. Hasemi must have had his mind on the job and was not being polite as George had to back off or be squished into the fence on the exit.

The race featured a fantastic battle between Grice and Brock at the sharp end and a spectacular rollover by Kevin Bartlett having oversteered into the wall at the top of the mountain due to a punctured rear tyre, finishing upside down.

It was another masterful Brock win and he finished a couple of laps ahead of Grice who was followed on the same lap by John Harvey's second HDT Commodore. The Janson/Parsons Commodore was fourth, Jim Richards in the 635 BMW fifth, and Moffat/Katayama sixth.

Some laps into the race Hasemi was running eighth and Fury eleventh and then not long after, ninth and tenth. At 30 mins in they were eighth and ninth, and at 20 laps Hasemi had just 21 seconds on Fury.

When Hasemi handed over to Hoshino they were in sixth outright and had been just five

Hasemi hands off to Hoshino, 4 tyres, full fuel, sub 40 secs.

seconds behind Moffat's RX-7. While #56 was in the pits Fury radioed in to say the Bluebird was overheating and he needed to come in. *"One more lap please George…"*, said Marsden, *"…56 is in."* The one more lap was too far though, as after he'd gone around again, George came in to retire with a blown head gasket.

Car #56's second stop was made a couple of laps early due to a punctured tyre but very soon after, they were back in with a very noisy universal joint in the RH drive shaft. Hasemi sat calm and focussed at the wheel for 14 minutes while the drive shaft was replaced, during which they slipped back to second in class. Hasemi very quickly hauled in the Capri though and left it in his wake, the two Japanese raced flat out for the rest of the day and, at the flag, were more than six laps ahead of second place in class B and eighth outright, ten laps down on Brock.

It was once again an incredible learning experience for us but it also crystallised our realisation that class successes had become irrelevant, we were from then on only shooting for the podium.

Endurance Championship Drivers' points following the James Hardie 1000 at Bathurst were: Parmenter (V6 Capri) 12, Johnson (Falcon) 10, Moffat 10, Morris (Falcon) 9, Brock (Commodore) 9, Gibson 9, Fury 6, McLeod (Strongbow RX-7) 4. Barry Seton (V6 Capri) 10. (*9-6-4-3-2-1 points awarded for each class)

And for the Manufacturers' title: Nissan 24, Ford 22, Toyota 21, Holden 17, Mazda 14, BMW 5. (*9-6-4-3-2-1 points awarded for the highest placed finisher in each class)

A post-race memory from Dave Thommo:

"The spares truck was a rented semi and the driver had taken off after arriving at Bathurst, saying he wasn't interested in car racing. Howard had a truck full of spares with no driver so I was lumbered with driving it home without the correct licence and many years since I had driven a Kenworth with a 12 speed roadranger box, Dennis unhappily for him was to be my jockey, I think it was 30-40 km before the gearbox stopped making those dreadful crunching noises.

There really was no time to relax with this thing, you had to be into it constantly to keep it flowing, Den was pretty nervous and wasn't very complimentary about my driving, insisting I stop at a bottle shop so he could have his own party tucked away in the sleeper-cab. I'm pretty sure we drove all night as I can remember arriving back in the driveway at Healey Rd in the early morning, much to Den's delight."

Maybe it was this episode that motivated Den to get his heavy licence for he became the driver of our Nissan UD prime mover from 1983 onward.

The repeat of a drive shaft failure also prompted George S. to go looking for a solution which led to the adoption of upgraded half shafts with Porsche CV joints from then on. See further info on this on page 166.

AEC Round 4 Gold Coast 300, Surfers Paradise Raceway, Qld, November 7

A rather thin field fronted up for Round 4 of the AEC at Surfers Paradise due to a planned special touring car race as a support for the Australian Grand Prix at Calder Park on the same weekend. The organisers of the AGP weekend were forced by CAMS to cancel this clashing support race at a late date but by then several Touring Car teams had opted out of attending the Queensland meeting. Nearly half of the cars to start were from the under 3-litre class. Leading the Manufacturers Title chase at that point in time we were a 'must run'.

Marsden, Gibson, Fury. Two of them were waiting to go out to the starting grid. Not the ideal backdrop for this pic.

In practice, Allan Moffat was best with a 1:15.8, Dick Johnson next with 1:16.1 then Fury would be on the outside of the front row with 1:16.5. On row two would be Barry Jones, also with 1:16.5 and Greg Hansford with 1:16.8. Fred Gibson could only manage a 1:19.2 to be fifteenth on the grid.

There was drama on the grid on the Sunday even before the flag was raised when Fred managed to stall the Bluebird. He sat in place as the field roared off on lap one. Johnson slightly bettered Fury to lead on the first lap by a whisker with Masterton two whiskers back in third. Moffat

Johnson - Fury - Masterton then daylight by the end of the back straight on the 1st lap.

had botched the launch and was back in sixth or seventh. Gibson finally got the Bluebird started and he trundled off after the field.

There followed 25 laps of close and exciting racing and position swapping by which time the ultimate positions had been established with Moffat, Fury and Johnson had cemented their places on the podium and were just waiting for them to set.

Fred in for a scheduled full service pit stop. One of the few races we ran Good Year tyres.

When the 95 laps had wound down Fury's Bluebird was the only car on the same lap as Moffat's winning Mazda with Johnson's Falcon down one lap, Shiel's Mazda down two, Masterton's Falcon down three and Gibson's Bluebird just on the same lap as Masterton, down three laps. Fury placed first and Gibson second in the 3-litre class with only daylight third.

Endurance Championship Drivers' points following the Gold Coast 300 were: Johnson (Falcon) 16, Gibson 15, Fury 15, Parmenter (V6 Capri) 13, Moffat 10, Barry Seton (V6 Capri) 10, Morris (Falcon) 9, Brock (Commodore) 9, McLeod (Strongbow RX-7) 4. (*9-6-4-3-2-1 points awarded for each class)

And for the Manufacturers' title: Nissan 33, Toyota 30, Ford 28, Mazda 23, Holden 19, BMW 5. (*9-6-4-3-2-1 points awarded for the highest placed finisher in each class).

AEC Round 5 Nissan-Datsun 300, Adelaide Raceway, SA, December 4-5

Most of the top contenders arrived for the final round out at Virginia on this hot December weekend and all were keen to get their quick laps done as soon as possible on Saturday morning to avoid the hottest part of the day. As was generally expected, Brock was fastest with a 58.3 but maybe not so expectedly Fury did a 58.4 which Moffat then matched placing the three of them on the front row of the starting grid for Sunday. Gibson won eighth place with a 59.9.

On Sunday Fury got a blinder off the line and was about four lengths ahead of Brock by halfway down the straight. He led until lap two – the first time a Bluebird had led a race – when Brock and then also Grice drove past on the long straight. On lap six Grice pushed passed Brock into the lead and looked to be moving away from the Brock, Fury, Moffat train.

Fury leaves Brock, Moffat and the rest in his dust at Adelaide.

As the big cars' tyres began to suffer and Moffat got the Mazda wound up, he managed to squeeze past Brock and then also Grice to take the lead, which he built on as the race progressed. Fury also got past Grice who seemed to be slowing, which was confirmed when he suddenly swerved across the paths of two following Commodores, making a late decision to dive into the pits due to a very noisy diff. Fury was also in trouble though and came to the pits with something amiss in the front suspension. He missed 10 laps while we battled to rectify a stripped thread on the top of the RH front strut[7] before he could re-join in seventh place – which he held to the finish. Car #56 began overheating late in the race and Gibson just managed to nurse it home in fourth place.

Endurance Championship Drivers' points at the end of the series

---

7   In order to swap front springs, the nut that retains the strut shaft in its top mount was continually being undone and done up again with the pneumatic 'rattle gun' – apparently once too often for this particular thread.

following the Nissan-Datsun 300 in Adelaide were: Allan Moffat 28, Bob Holden (running in the 1600 to 2-litre class) 26, Fred Gibson 24, George Fury 21, Dick Johnson 16, Peter Brock 15, Brian Parmenter 13, Allan Grice 12, Barry Seton (V6 Capri) 10, Bob Morris (Falcon) 9, Masahiro Hasemi 9. (*9-6-4-3-2-1 points awarded for each class)

And for the Manufacturers' title: Nissan 42, Ford 37, Mazda 32, Toyota 30, Holden 25. (*9-6-4-3-2-1 points awarded for the highest placed finisher in each class)

So a championship title for us – a shame nobody seemed to care two hoots about the Australian Endurance Championship for makes. Ho hum.

It must have been galling for Nissan after declaring that the Bluebird racing program was initiated to promote and publicise the name change from Datsun, to hear race commentators, and read motoring journalists' stories a full year into the program, continuing to refer to our cars as Datsuns. This even though the name Nissan was the only prominent name showing on the cars – front, back and sides.

Late 1983, Den helping the modellers smooth the clay from which a mould was taken to produce the new fibreglass front.

1983

A rather uncomfortable split had developed in our team and resources were further divided between Sydney (Fred Gibson's Road & Track business) and our Dandenong South workshop in Melbourne.

Maybe this could be seen as mirroring the split that had developed between the Australian Touring Car Championship and the AMSCAR series for touring car dominance in Australia.

Howard was nothing if not a very clever schemer though and we're pretty sure the story we were told was that Fred would use the Amaroo-based AMSCAR series for development while we'd get on with the business of trying to win the ATCC series with George. Thinking about it with hindsight though, I reckon there was more to it than that...

We received our beautiful, spanking-new Pantech with Nissan Diesel prime mover about this time, fortunately kept in Melbourne or there may have been a revolt. It would carry both race cars, had pull-out ramps,

Truckin' Life Magazine 'Rig of the Month' poster supplement.

a winch for pulling the cars in, all sorts of storage including for up to about 40 wheels and tyres, beautiful aluminium work benches (that saw

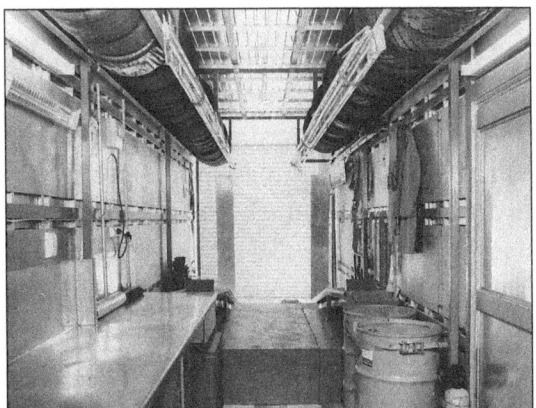

Inside the pantec. A lift out ramp exposes fuel drums. On the other side a wall heater and a very functional work bench. See minimum ground clearance gauge next to broom at left!

many a turbocharger rebuild) and the floor was finished with black and white vinyl tiles. Just brilliant. Dennis had got his heavy vehicle licence and he did a brilliant job of getting our mobile workshop, together with the race cars, all over the country until the end of the Bluebird program.

Even though its events interleave with the ATCC rounds, I've again chosen to cover the AMSCAR series separately here so as not to break into the more exciting ATCC series, which is covered next.

1983 AMSCAR Better Brakes series, Amaroo Park

As per 1982, the AMSCAR series was fully televised and had good prize money, the slightly changed concept for 1983 though was of practice and qualifying on the Saturday and then three 10-lap races on the Sunday. The four rounds were held on March 6, April 10, May 22 and July 10.

I reckon Howard's thinking was to have a team running in each of the two competing series – he could keep us apart somewhat while multiplying Nissan's chance of successes.

What eventuated was a Terry Shiel domination of the series in his Mazda RX-7 with wins in March, April and July. Gibson won the round held in May.

AMSCAR Round 1, March 6

On a 40 degree day Fred had promisingly put his Bluebird on pole but, late in practice, had broken its tail shaft. In the short, un-timed practice session on the equally hot Sunday morning, the replacement tail shaft also broke. So, maybe because there was no second spare, HM had to announce that Fred would be a non-starter for any of the heats that day.

All three heats produced tight racing with plenty of biff, bash and heat-related frailties to amuse the crowd that braved the weather. Grice was at his un-conceding best (or was it worst), Johnson's Falcon seemed unwilling to respond to the helm and Masterton raised the ire of the stewards, not only for his part in an on-track incident with Grice's Commodore but for knowingly presenting an illegal car – his team had installed a spring loaded flap in the front bumper which would open backwards at speed to allow more air to the radiator. He was fined $1000, given a one-week licence suspension, and was excluded from Round 2. A bit harsh for 'just a bit of fun'.

Shiel took the points.

AMSCAR Round 2, April 10

Saturday Practice for Round 2, in much more comfortable weather, produced a very impressive lap of 52.4 for Terry Shiel, 1.1 seconds under his own previous lap record! Jones wasn't much slower, doing a 52.6 and then Fred did a 53.3 to claim third place on the grid.

Once again, for the first heat, Gibson failed to take his place on the grid due apparently to a broken half shaft in the rear. In another hard-fought and entertaining race, Shiel beat Jones home by less than a second with Grice a further five seconds back.

Fred finally made it to the start of the second heat and began quite well to be fourth behind Masterton at the top of the hill on lap 1. He disposed of the big Falcon in fairly short order but was never able to get close to the very quick RX-7s. Jones, Shiel, daylight, Gibson.

There was an amusing interview with Fred and Howard telecast between heats during which, when asked if the cars had potential to further improve, HM said *"yes, for both cars and drivers"* and then, in relation to the V8 cars, said *"there must have been a time when there were still some dinosaurs lingering after all the others were gone."* Mike Raymond, after a sideways glance at Fred, picked up on HM's comment about getting more from the drivers and asked Fred if he'd been slacking off again. Fred, embarrassed, replied *"no, he was working hard on his fitness..."* forcing HM to interject and back away from his statement about the drivers with a typical piece of HM reframing that didn't really hit the mark, saying that *"Fred in particular likes a 'good' car... he'll be faster in a well setup car..."* An interesting comment considering the commentators had been calling Fred, 'Nissan's Development and Racing Driver'.

Anyway, in the third heat, Jones faltered off the line slightly, blocking Shiel and allowing Gibson into the lead, which he held for half a lap then unaccountably ran two wheels off the track and lost about five places – maybe he was fumbling trying to reach the boost adjuster, haha. He clawed back up to third and was challenging Grice for second but got tangled up with Masterton on the final corner, hit the wall and was fortunate to get across the finish the line for fourth. Shiel, Grice, Masterton, Gibson.

AMSCAR Round 3, May 22

In the respected Australian Motor Racing Yearbook the story of this weekend begins: *"Nissan team driver Fred Gibson made Australian motor racing history at Amaroo Park on May 22 by winning the third round of the Better Brakes AMSCAR series. Gibson's factory Bluebird Turbo won two of the three 10-lap heats and was second in the other, giving him overall victory. It was the first 'major' win by a turbocharged car in local touring car racing – and a world-class success for the Bluebird Turbo."*

Well, what can I say? If this para wasn't written by Fred Gibson, it must have been Howard Marsden. Major win? World-class success? Come now!

It went on to say: *"The result also had great personal significance for Gibson. It was the pay-off for the Bluebird Turbo's 18 months of development work, the bulk of which has been done by the 42-year-old Sydney veteran. The win also ended Gibson's 10-year absence from the winner's circle in major-league racing – his previous big victory was back in 1973 in an endurance race at Adelaide International Raceway driving an XA Falcon Hardtop."* Sheesh!

So, Saturday Practice, to kick off what would be a very wet weekend, saw Fred, no doubt running a new set of Marsden's best wet-weather tyres, fastest with a 1:57.8 to Jones 1:57.9 and a good break over the rest who, I'm imagining, would have dusted off their crusty 5-year old wets for the occasion.

Light rain was falling as they headed off on heat one. Fred muffed the start and was fourth as they completed lap 1. He recovered to return to second place early in the race and while he caught up to Jones he could not find a way to pass before the finish. Jones first, Gibson second, Finnigan third, Shiel fourth.

Very close but no cigar for Fred in Heat 1 at Round 3.

No rain for heat two but a still greasy surface.

Gibson got a good start but Jones a better one. Fred got past him coming onto the straight and then suddenly there was carnage everywhere with about six cars involved so Fred was left way out in front unchallenged, with McLeod second and Wilmington's Falcon third, and that's how it finished.

Heat three was run in heavy rain and with a darkening sky, a much-reduced field lined up due to the heat two carnage. Gibson (on full wets) jumped well and was first into turn 1, going away. Fred cruised to a very easy win with Jones' and McLeod's RX-7s second and third.

Now I ask you, was there anything I missed there that would suggest this was a world-class success? I must apologise for the cynicism but to suggest that Fred had done the bulk of the development and testing to that stage was absolutely ludicrous – South Dandenong was where all the serious engineering and development happened and Calder where George Fury did the meaningful test driving.

By this time for instance we'd worked out the problem with the front end of the car and re-engineered it to cure the migrating roll centre, allowing the use of 450 lb front springs and transforming the handling (read more about this on page 158). It was irksome at best to read the press release above knowing what was told to us at the coalface at the time.

At least his win here produced a laurel for Fred to rest on, as he never again made it onto the podium.

AMSCAR Round 4, July 10

A return to fine and dry conditions was welcome for most of the crews that managed to return for Round 4 of the series. The EXA Turbo build was well under way in Melbourne so it was decided Christine Gibson should be given an opportunity to dust off the cobwebs and accordingly Bluebird #55 was taken to Sydney for her. However, again from the Australian Motor Racing Yearbook: *"Once again the entry was generally mediocre – it's strange how the Moffats, Brocks, Johnsons and even Grices avoid this series..."*

In practice Barry Jones recorded an amazing 52.0 seconds to grab pole, Shiel was next best with a 52.5 and then Gibson and Willmington both with a best times of 53.5. Mrs Gibson's 55.6 was good enough only for eleventh place on the grid. Only 14 cars faced the starter.

In heat one, Fred was fifth into turn 1, Christine 10th. At the end of lap 1, Jones led Shiel followed by Wilmington's Falcon then Fred, who'd gotten past Finnigan's Commodore. The telecast didn't show why but Wilmington's XD Falcon dropped out and Finnigan re-passed Fred, then the two cars that had deservedly hogged the TV coverage, Jones and Shiel switched places on the last lap. We never saw #56 on the telecast after lap 1. Shiel, Jones, Finnigan, Gibson.

In heat two, Jones' engine failed just after he dropped the clutch for the start and Wilmington got a flier to lead Shiel, Finnigan and Gibson. Mid race, Shiel managed to get passed the Falcon and proceeded to leave it for dead. Then, late in the race, both Finnigan and Fiery Fred (christened by commentator Gary Wilkinson) also got past Wilmington. Christine in #55 was seen on the telecast at one stage for about 5 seconds. At the end, Shiel, Finnigan, F. Gibson, Gary Wilmington.

In heat three, Fred made a better start and was only three or four lengths behind Shiel coming out of turn 1 but nearly surrounded by Commodores and Falcons. Fiery lived up to his new name late in the race when his turbocharger let go in a big way as he was accelerating out of Wunderlich Corner onto pit straight and he was lost in a huge cloud of oily smoke as he coasted to stop just past the pits and caught fire. Luckily there were fire marshals handy and able to put him out.

We later found that the turbine wheel had smashed its way out of the turbine housing to escape down the dump pipe. The stainless steel pipe did a 90° turn to exit under the car's sill but the turbine wheel failed to take the turn, in stead puncturing the pipe and lodging in its wall.

Some turbo failures were more dramatic than others, this one I think our most explosive. It was a good thing the near white hot wheel, travelling at considerable speed, lodged itself in the wall of the exhaust pipe rather than in soft tissue in the pit lane or we may have been banned from Australian circuits then and there.

Christine warmed to the task and in the last heat of the day managed to bring BB2 home in fourth place in a rather depleted field.

Terry Shiel though had won each heat on the day and took the points for Round 4 as well as the Championship.

In the end, for Nissan the 1983 AMSCAR Series seemed quite a lot of effort for very little as Shiel dominated the series and captured most of the TV exposure for Mazda – Nissan received very little as Fred failed to start in four of the 12 races and, other than winning two heats on the very wet and gloomy afternoon of the third round, seemed seldom involved in the race drama and was thus little seen on the telecasts.

Mazda was the big winner, albeit in a car that really should have been racing in one of the sports car series. HM's gaff and embarrassing back-pedal in his pit interview with Mike Raymond wouldn't have helped much either. I wasn't there and don't remember what was learned – hopefully there was some upside.

1983 AUSTRALIAN TOURING CAR CHAMPIONSHIP

The 1983 Australian Touring Car Championship was, by way of contrast, an engrossing series, fully supported by all the big teams and name drivers and featured a fiercely-fought battle between Grice and Moffat. From our perspective though, it was notable for our outright competitiveness and the reliability of the Bluebird, as well as for the pride we felt both for George and our cars in at last being fully recognized as leading contenders in the circus, and mostly even called Nissans! It would prove to be the Bluebird's best series in terms of consistent results.

1983 also marked the change to this series being telecast by the ABC, resulting in a very welcome enhanced TV coverage.

The other thing I can't forget about the '83 ATCC was the escalating decibels from the quick RX-7s – it was literally very painful to be on the pit wall without good ear protection.

Controversy swirled throughout the series, with some teams, notably the MHDT (Brock) and STP Roadways (Grice) claiming that Moffat was foxing during the championship in an effort to 'hoodwink' CAMS into believing the RX-7s, which ran the 1.2 litre 12A rotary engine, needed the larger and more powerful 1.3 litre 13B engine in order to be competitive against the V8's at Bathurst. Ultimately CAMS approved the 13B (as well as the late approval also of fuel injection), but also granted concessions to the Commodore's and Falcons, which ended up giving them an even larger advantage over the RX-7s and put our Nissan Bluebirds at further *dis*advantage.

Fury at Calder beginning his most successful ATCC series. This the only race without a background for the numbers.

Round 1 Calder Park Raceway, Keilor, Victoria, February 5-6

This was the last race the Bluebirds would do with the small (optional road car) rear spoiler. Den had been busy at our workshop adapting a much larger Commodore one he'd managed to purloin and which debuted at Sandown, two weeks later.

The entry list for this race was the best for a number of years with all the big names showing their intention to battle out this championship.

February 5-6 was a very hot weekend as Melbourne can certainly deliver at that time of year, especially in Melbourne's wind-swept outer western suburbs.

Grice did best in practice with his brand new STP Roadways VH Commodore SS, challenging the rest with a record breaking 44.83 seconds. Moffat was able to do a 45.08, good enough to also win himself a spot on the front row. Brock qualified third with a 45.22 and Fury announced our team's improvements with a 45.30, as did Fiery Fred with a 45.50.

Johnson, who'd been battling handling issues with his XE Falcon and co-opted George Shepheard to help sort it, indicated he was beginning to get somewhere with his 45.77 and completed the top six, all of whom were under Calder Park's Touring Car lap record.

Grice leads but Fury best of the rest here at the Esses.

Come the start on Sunday, Grice and Fury got away best, George demonstrating his skill at getting the turbo wound up on the grid. Brock and Moffat were a bit tardy, the former sliding off in turn 1 when his brakes weren't up to temperature and wouldn't perform. Gibson didn't get away at all as his gearbox broke when he dumped the clutch. He was soon push-started though and went on to complete the race with only fourth and fifth gears.

Back at the startline after the first lap it was Grice, Fury, Moffat, Johnson, Cullen, Rogers, Harrington, Masterton, Carter, Brock, which provided 10 laps or so of very exciting racing with all sorts of position changes. Suddenly though, Grice slewed sideways and slowed – his bottom radiator hose had been damaged by his harmonic balancer coming adrift and he'd slipped in his own coolant. He stopped when he saw his temp gauge hit the red.

This left Fury in the lead but he soon needed to back off as the Bluebird's engine temperature was also way high, letting Moffat and then also Brock past, Brock having past nine cars in his recovery! Johnson soon gave up his battle to keep the big Ford engine from overheating as did Masterton a few laps later.

Brock's gearbox failed on lap 30 ending an heroic drive and leaving Moffat in the clear out front. Moffat went on to lap every car remaining in the race other than Fury's Bluebird. Murray Carter placed third and Gibson, who'd spent most of the race in around thirteenth place, ended up a creditable seventh, two laps down.

The results from this race exposed a major flaw in CAMS' new points scoring system (25-23-20-17-15-13-11-10-9-8-7-etc. but with bonus points for up to 3000cc cars in these outright places of: 5-4-4-4-4, etc.) whereby Fury scored 27 points for placing second to Moffat's 25 points for his win. This was a little embarrassing for our team as we'd pretty much forgotten by then that we were still officially running in the up to 3-litre class. We didn't give the points back though. After the Calder round, scores were: Fury 27, Moffat 25, Carter (Falcon) 20, Cullen (Commodore) 15.

CAMS resolved this problem at the completion of the ATCC series by changing the turbocharged equivalency ratio from 1.4:1 to a suspiciously contrived 1.7:1, thereby pushing us into the over 3-litre class (from 2478cc to 3009cc).

ATCC Round 2 Sandown Raceway, Melbourne, Victoria, February 19-20

Practice got under way in very hot and hazy conditions due to bushfires (smoke from Cockatoo in the Dandenongs, just 15kms away, could be clearly seen on the horizon). The promised upgrades to the Sandown circuit had not materialized and the track was unchanged.

Brock, who'd been absent, awaiting the birth of his daughter, arrived just in time in the final practice session to put his car in pole position with a 1:11.4. Fury did a 1:11:9 to win the other front row slot, then Grice in the still very new looking STP Roadways Commodore just one tenth of a second back on the third row beside Johnson, who'd really struggled with his Falcon to do a 1:12.4. Moffat did a mid-12s in his LHD[1] RX-7 to get the inside run on row three, beside Gibson who'd managed a 1:12:8.

Fury once again made a great start and led the race to the kink coming onto the back straight but was then gobbled up by Brock and then Grice on the way up to the top of the circuit. George then had a very near miss coming under Dunlop Bridge. He clipped the kerb on the entry to the bend and the Bluebird was well and truly up on two wheels at about 140kmh and came oh-so-close to collecting the Armco. It would have been a very big crash but only resulted in him being passed by Johnson, and then, on the second lap, he was also passed by Moffat.

Grice's Commodore seemed to have been better set up for the track – either handling or gearing – as he was clearly faster everywhere but on the straights and after he squeezed past he drove away from Brock.

As the race settled it was Grice with a safe buffer to Brock then Johnson then Fury with Rogers, Carter and Gibson following in a bunch. Then, on lap 14, Gibson tapped the back of Carter's Falcon and damaged his radiator. He'd obviously been too busy to look at his coolant temp gauge because the engine finally stopped on the back straight.

ARCO cnr, Fury wanting past Johnson's too wide Falcon.

Brock had slowed somewhat and Moffat had been able to get passed then set off after Grice. With six laps to go, Moffat tried a desperate late braking pass around the outside of Grice at the end of the pit straight but with rear end hopping up and down over the ripples the Mazda broke an axle and retired on the exit to the corner.

Grice won, Brock second, Johnson third and Fury fourth, all over the back of Johnson's Falcon for many laps but unable to find a way past, due mostly to Sandown's two long straights. Carter cruised home in fifth.

---

1   Moffat had both a right and a left hand drive RX-7 and depending on whether the circuit ran clockwise or counter clockwise he would bring the one that had him on the inside most corners. Head-shakingly this was within the regulations at that time.

Following Sandown, ATCC scores were: Fury 48, Carter 35, Harrington 26, Moffat 25, Cullen 24.

ATCC Round 3 Symmons Plains Raceway, Launceston, Tas., March 12-13

We only sent BB2 (55) across Bass straight in the transporter in 1983 – it would have left about the same time as Round 1 of the AMSCAR series was run.

This was 40 laps of the 2.41 km circuit, very hard on brakes. It was George's first time at Symmons Plains and the Bluebird was not handling to his liking. Moffat took his LHD car for this counter-clockwise circuit.

Grice won pole with an early first session lap of 58:93 seconds, Moffat won the other front row spot with 59:18, then Brock, who was recovering from pleurisy, on 59:31, Fury 59:65, and Johnson 1:00:16. Local boy David Parsons did well with a next best of 1:00.66 in his unsupported Commodore. Six cars were under the existing lap record.

All got away cleanly at the start, but Fury got the power down best and he led into turn 1 but was then gobbled up on the back straight by Grice and Brock. Eight laps later Moffat also got past Fury, so that at lap 10 it was Grice, Brock, Moffat, Fury, Parsons, Johnson. Once the race settled down, the main

This time, at Symmons, it's Moffat holding George up.

attraction was Moffat's progress through the field, first getting past Brock, whose brakes were starting to look suspect, and then reeling in Grice.

On lap 33, George did a good job of getting past Brock under brakes and took over third place only to see Brock retire on the following lap. Grice and Moffat swapped the lead several times and in the process Moffat got muscled off, giving Grice enough lead to hang onto till the end. So, after a thrilling race, the final result was Grice about 1 second to the good of Moffat who was about 20 seconds ahead of Fury, with Parsons a similar distance behind.

At the end of the weekend George led the series on 72 to Grice on 50 and Moffat on 48.

ATCC Round 4 Wanneroo Park, Perth, Western Australia, April 20-21

Our first trip to Wanneroo! We'd arrived on the Tuesday and put in four good days of car sorting, blemished only by a single turbo failure on the Friday. At the close of Saturday's qualifying, Dick Johnson had pole position on the grid with a 62.46 followed by Allan Moffat with 62.55, Peter Brock with 62.56, Allan Grice on 62.73 and George Fury on 62.94 – all under the lap record! It promised an exciting 35-lap race.

On a stunning, blue-sky day Moffat got a great start and was challenging for the lead in turn 1. As they arrived back at the main straight though, it was Johnson with a clear lead – Brock and Moffat, battling for second. Grice had got past Fury to be fourth. The scrap between those first five on the opening laps was thrilling.

Fury got back past Grice but it soon became evident the STP Commodore was in trouble and he headed to the pits trailing blue smoke. Moffat was all over the back of Brock, and Fury battled with Johnson a couple of seconds back from the leading duel. Johnson's tyres began to fade and Fury was able to get past and make it a rip-roaring threesome at the front.

Brock, Moffat, Fury, dicing hard and keeping the fans on their toes, both local and on the TV.

Moffat had begun with a light fuel load and on lap 16 darted into the pits for a very rapid stop (just 11 seconds), resuming in third place. The Mazda then, in very few laps, proceeded to reel in the Bluebird and the red and white Commodore, giving us a short glimpse of the RX-7's true speed. Brock, Moffat and Fury were dicing furiously – very entertaining – and then Brock lost traction under hard braking and spun, holding up Moffat and allowing Fury through to lead again on lap 28. Brock was left behind bogged in the sand. Moffat once again quickly caught Fury and took back the lead, drawing away to win by 3.4 seconds. Johnson was third about 18 second in arrears. Brock came home in ninth place after finally de-bogging the Commodore.

Moffat's light fuel load and early pitstop were discussed and argued over for months afterward with one side of the fence insisting it was a sham in an effort to strengthen his claim for further allowances from CAMS. He'd been able to take a second and a half per lap from Brock after his pretended pit stop!

Progressive scores in the ATCC at the end of the Wanneroo weekend were Fury 99, Moffat 73, Harrington (STP Commodore) 56, Johnson 55, Grice (STP Commodore) 50. Brock was 9th with just 32 points.

Round 5 The Mazda 100, Adelaide Raceway, South Australia, May 1

On another cracker of a weekend, Moffat, this time in his right-hand-drive Stuyvesant RX-7, grabbed pole position with a 57.4. Fury, a full two seconds quicker than his previous best at Adelaide in 1982, and despite sacrificing another turbocharger, put our #55 Bluebird alongside Moff on the front row of the grid with a 57.8. Brock was later able to match Fury's time so he completed the front row. Grice got the inside of the second row with 58.0 and had Johnson alongside, credited with a 58.4. Harrington did a 58.9 to make the top six all under the old lap record.

In front of 10,000+ yelling fans Adelaide Flag Marshal Glen Dix, got the field away to a clean start for the 40-lapper.

Off to pay a visit to the AIR scrutineers, muscle included!

After the long drag down to turn 1, it was Brock, Moffat, Grice (who'd characteristically pushed his way in to the single file entry) then Fury, with Johnson back in eighth. As things settled, Brock had a small lead from the tight bunch of Grice, Moffat and Fury, all battling hard. Moffat, who seemed to be able to find an extra gear when needed, tried to get past Grice but he pushed back and they touched and both nearly came to grief at the end of the straight. Fury tried to take advantage but Grice pushed him off as well – almost a big mess. Moffat repeated the same manoeuvre on the next lap and this time managed to get past.

So it was Brock out front with Moffat, Grice and Fury under the one blanket. Places were swapped several times and at one stage Fury managed to get under both Grice and Moffat to take second, which he was able to hold for just two laps. Moffat and Grice slowly caught up and then Moffat darted out of the slipstream and nailed Fury at the end of the main straight. Fury began locking the LH rear on the off-camber bit of the track where it turns onto the bowl. The three of them were nose to tail once again.

By lap 25 the race had settled somewhat with Brock, Moffat, Grice, Fury holding reasonably comfortable positions although Moffat was beginning to close in on Brock. With 10 laps to go Moffat caught Brock and there followed 10 minutes of brilliant, close and clean racing with Moffat not quite able to get past, although they were often alongside each other coming onto the front straight.

At one point in the race where Moffat was closing in on Brock for the lead, the yellow flags came out due to an incident where one of the mid-field-running Commodores slid off the track. While most backed off a notch, Moff kept the pedal to the metal and caught right up on Brock's tail. He was shown the 'bad sportsmanship' flag but, as per normal, while he usually showed respect to his fellow competitors, he ignored the signal.

There was high drama on the last lap, as Cullen, being lapped but maybe unaware of the hotly contested dual behind, would not give way. Narrowly avoiding more than one disaster, Moffat and Brock came through the last corner side by side for a photo finish. Brock got it, just half a bumper bar ahead of Moffat then, nine seconds adrift, came Grice with Fury another four seconds behind him. It had been another exciting and dramatic race featuring the closest ever finish.

This was not the first time that the normally mind-mannered Moffat had been disparaging of Grice's driving in post-race interviews but this time viewers really knew he was pissed, maybe with Commodore drivers in general.

Championship points at end of Round 5 were Fury 120, Moffat 96, Johnson and Grice equal third on 70 and Brock on 57. If Fury dropped his worst score (as was required) he'd still be leading on 99 points.

Round 6 Surfers Paradise Raceway, Gold Coast, Queensland, May 14-15

Whereas the 1983 AMSCAR Series was affected by one extremely hot round and another extremely wet one, the weather gods smiled on the ATCC in '83 – we were treated to another pleasant, warm weekend on the Gold Coast and again the fans turned out in droves.

Moffat obviously had his eyes on the championship by this stage as, for the last three rounds, he ran a two-car team hoping to push Fury down an extra place in the finishing order. Spoiler alert: The plan worked a treat.

Practice for Round 6. Damn, there goes another turbocharger.

Pole position was again captured by Moffat in his RHD RX-7 with a 1:14.2, followed by Brock with a 1:14.6, then Greg Hansford in the second RHD Stuyvesant RX-7 on 1:14.8. Next was Allan Grice's STP Commodore with 1:14.8 and then George Fury in Car #55 on 1:15.1, to the disappointment no doubt of the provincial crowd, a full .8 of a second ahead of local hero Dick Johnson in the Palmer Tube Mills Falcon on 1:15.9.

Brock got a great start on Sunday and at the end of lap 1 of 30, was several seconds ahead of a furious duel between Grice and Moffat and with Johnson and Fury close behind. Meanwhile Hansford had made a very poor start, nearly stalling the Mazda to be eighth at laps end. Johnson slowed and retired to the pits on lap 2, apparently with a gearbox problem. Moffat battled with Brock for first, Fury battled with Grice for many laps for third and fourth, and Hansford and Harrington continuously swapped 5th and 6th.

Moffat took the lead from Brock at half distance and about the same time, Fury took third from Grice. Five laps later both Commodores retook their recently lost positions, but not for long. With just three laps to go, for unknown reasons, Grice drove into the pits not to re-emerge. Hansford, who'd gradually advanced through the ranks, arrived on Fury's tail with two laps to go and managed to thread the needle through a narrowing gap between the Bluebird and the pit wall on the main straight.

Not able to match Hansford's speed, George tried to put the squeeze on but to no avail, he was through and gone.

Dicing with our nemesis to no avail once again.

So, as the brilliant, hard-fought and exciting race wound down and with Moffat slowing to pretend everything was still pretty close between the cars, Brock was closing in. Moffat had things under control though and engineered a reversal of the Adelaide race finish, winning by 0.2 of a second. Hansford took third from George, fulfilling Moffat's goal of denying Fury points. A shame we didn't yet have Gary Scott on board.

The ATCC score card after the race had Fury still leading on 141 points (but needing to drop one result, the lowest available being one of his 23s), followed by Moffat on 121, Brock on 80, Harrington on 75 and then Grice and Johnson both on 70.

Round 7 Oran Park Raceway, Sydney, N.S.W, May 28-29

Round 7 was on Oran Park's brilliant, although difficult to pass at, longer (Grand Prix) track. Howard was in Japan on company business and did not attend.

Fury took pole position with a 1:15.2 lap (2.2 seconds under the lap record at the time). Sharing the front row would be Moffat who managed a 1:15.7, followed by Brock with a 1:16.1, Grice with a 1:16.4, Shiel (RX-7) with a 1:16.7, and Johnson who was able to do a 1:17.1, despite his handling problems with the heavy Falcon. Gibson managed a 1:18.5 to achieve 13th grid position in the back half of the field at this, his other home circuit. It was at this meeting where Fred decided the Bluebird was just too scary to drive and that he should retire.

Between qualifying and race it was decided to make a tweak to the rear suspension settings of George's car and also to use the soft compound tyres for the race. We survivors have no memory of whether Fred Gibson took responsibility for these decisions, though he would have been the ranking general in Howard's absence. They did not turn out well.

At the Sunday start of the 32-lap race, with yet another huge crowd in attendance, George needed a second dump of the clutch[2] and so did not start well. At turn 1 it was Brock, who'd begun brilliantly, followed by Moffat, Grice, Fury and Johnson, who proceeded to whack the fence on turn 3 and had to retire. Moffat was all over the back of Brock once again from the second lap and behind these two, Fury was harrying Grice, and Jones (RX-7) was challenging them both. On lap 7 Moffat did what had previously been thought impossible and passed Brock around the outside at the dogleg and slipped into first place. Looking back one commentator remarked that it was this move that was decisive in his winning the '83 championship.

At about this point in the race, rule changes for the Endurance Championship Series were announced on the TV telecast, and specifications detailed on-screen for viewers. These were to come into effect on August 1st. For cars 1200 to 1300Kgs (Commodore and BMW), wheel rims increased to 15"x12", cars over 1300Kg (Falcon, Camaro, Jaguar) wheels, including fitted tyres, raised to 16" width, Johnson allowed to run his requested new inlet manifold, Brock was denied his bigger brakes as CAMS said "he didn't ask for them", but would be allowed to reapply come July, the BMW 635 and also the Toyota Celica running in the 3-litre class, would be allowed to run the 24-valve cylinder heads they'd been asking for (in the case of the BMW apparently worth 50 bhp and about two seconds at Amaroo). For the RX-7s, they could use the bigger 13B engine.

For Nissan, only bad news, the turbo equivalency ratio was to be changed so we'd be running in the outright class from the beginning of the Endurance series and would loose our under 3-litre bonus points, although we could take advantage of the larger rim sizes commensurate with the Bluebird's weight. CAMS also said that if any car achieved dominance as a result of these new freedoms, they would immediately have weight penalties applied.

Following the mid-race announcement CAMS Chief Steward, John Large (who readers may remember was Ross Dunkerton's navigator for

---

2   To start a race well one needed to master the art of having the revs high enough so that when the clutch pedal is side-stepped there is enough instant power to spin the drive wheels sufficiently to accelerate away. Too much and the car sits there spinning its wheels, too little and the engine bogs down. A turbocharged car must be held firmly in place with the brakes to produce the load required to get the turbo spinning as well. This requires some fancy footwork as all three pedals need be accurately co-ordinated.

1973-74 and who was particularly disgruntled that he and Ross were denied works support after having done so well for Datsun on their own dime) was interviewed on-screen, saying "CAMS were only trying to even up the competition" – crikey, how much closer did they want it?! Controversy would swirl anew from that announcement.

So, receiving almost nothing from the announcement, other than this punch in the solar plexus, Fury (although he'd not felt the punch by then) was passed by Jones in the RX-7 to go back to fifth. The Bluebird looked rather tail happy by half distance (due apparently to the last-minute change to the rear suspension and the decision to run soft compound tyres for the first time) and in the second half of the race Fury was lapping slower and slower with tyres clearly past their best. It didn't matter so much though as everyone had to discard their lowest placing and this was, from half distance, clearly going to be it.

After Moffat achieved a lead of five seconds by around lap 10, he relaxed and held that until the last lap when he backed off a little more, letting Brock to within two seconds. So, it was Moffat then Brock then Grice about 10 seconds further back and they were followed closely by Barry Jones (RX-7) then another 10 seconds or so back to Fury in fifth place. Gibson finished 10th and, other than a very distant view on the grid, he was never sighted in the TV coverage and never mentioned in the commentary.

It was an easy win for Moffat and a fairly undramatic race – more drama coming from the CAMS announcement than from the track. At the post-race interviews it was apparent Moffat knew all about the freedoms granted to all competitors whereas Brock knew nothing at all of it and was clearly unhappy, both that most competitors were last to hear about the changes and also to hear Moffat would be free to run the 13B engine.

On reflection, I guess this is the treatment you got from CAMS when you had an English gentleman as your advocate. The rest of the team captains were not the 'kid gloves' types and would have been very squeaky hinges.

After this the penultimate race of the series, Fury was the only driver, and the #55 Bluebird the only car, to have done **every** lap of **every** race. The points standing at this stage showed Moffat on 146 points and Fury leading with 160 points but needing to drop his worst score – which at that stage was his 19 points from the sixth round. He could still win the series if he won the final race (171) and Moffat were to finish second (169) or lower.

Howard chose this point in time to get serious about our raw deal from CAMS and he withdrew our team from the final ATCC round allegedly in protest, although feeling the need to also give the excuse that we *"needed the time for further development before the Endurance Championship"!* How he explained this decision to George was something else again. And anyway, he reasoned to anyone enquiring, Fury's chances of beating Moffat at Lakeside weren't good.

Nissan's 'boycott' of the last round meant that George was required to forfeit his best chance of winning an ATCC championship and of becoming only the second driver, after Colin Bond, to win both the ATCC and the Australian Rally Championship.

Despite this, outside our core team (and probably within it if we'd been able to put aside our loyalties and ignore all the controversy over eligibility and legality) it was generally felt that justice had been served as Moffat and his RX-7 were usually the fastest combination. He'd only failed to finish once in the series and finished every other race on the podium, including four wins. He'd also had four pole positions and five fastest laps resulting in new lap records at Sandown, Symmons Plains, Wanneroo, Surfers (shared with Brock) and Oran Park. Fury's best were two seconds (Calder and Wanneroo) and one third (Symmons Plains).

Round 8 Lakeside Raceway, Brisbane, Queensland, June 18-19

As if reflecting the mood of many of the teams, grey skies and frequent showers greeted those that fronted up for the final round. It proved to be a rather lacklustre and disappointing end to what had been a wonderfully exciting series.

Moffat took pole position with a 1:00.6 on a soggy circuit after 150mm of overnight rain. Next was Johnson in his XE Falcon who equalled Moffat's time to share the front row of the grid. Third on the grid was Brock with a 1:01.3 followed by Hansford in the second Stuyvesant RX-7 with 1:02.3, and John English in an XD Falcon with 1:04.6.

Though a miserable day with intermittent showers 8000 fans turned up to watch what they hoped would be 35 laps of exciting racing. Hoping to receive a sign from the heavens all the heroes left it to the last minute to choose their tyres but in the end they all started on intermediates with fingers crossed.

On Sunday Moffat got off the line well and led into turn 1 with Brock and Johnson mixing it behind. Brock was forced wide and ran out of bitumen, then got completely sideways coming back onto the track and, if not for some brilliant evasion by Johnson, would have caused a huge pile up.

Everyone survived unscathed though and within the same lap, Brock got by Moffat who was driving gently with the title on the line and no doubt wanting CAMS to think they'd done the right thing in allowing the bigger engine. Johnson, who'd thought his power-steering pump had failed on the warm up lap but thought he could battle through without it, found instead that the power assist was intermittent, making his control of the helm most challenging. After what must have been a particularly unnerving slide through Hungry Corner on lap 5 he decided to call it quits.

So demurely was Moffat proceeding that after just 10 laps, Brock had passed and built up an 18 second lead, and that was to Greg Hansford who'd passed his boss and left him behind!

There was no further change to positions after 20 laps except that Brock was getting close to lapping Moffat and did so on lap 23. On the 35th and final lap Brock also lapped second-placed Gregg Hansford adding that ignominy to his total domination of the event and the conditions in which it was run.

Despite his uninspiring Sunday drive, Moffat, down nearly two laps, finished third giving him a winning total of 166 points in the championship to Fury's 160. It could well have been a very different story but for HM's decision for the team to boycott this eighth and final round as George was always reliably quick in the wet.

Brock finished the series third with 128 points, Grice fourth with 90, Harrington sixth with 72, and Johnson, disappointingly seventh after dominating the ATCC in 1982, with 70.

I believe it was while the other teams were at Lakeside that we came up with a mark II version of the transverse linked rear suspension. The fabricated steel 'box' attached to the diff housing, to which the arms attached, had cracked so Pete Anderson came up with the clever idea of two aluminium plates, one between the diff housing and its rear cover and the other behind the cover, as the inner mount for the rear transverse arms. See photo and a full description on page 164.

Over the break between series, finishing work was done on the new front bodywork – distinguished by the fully white bumper bars integrated with the spoiler. Clay modellers came and worked in our western workshop, spending weeks transforming Paul Beranger's design drawings into 3-dimensional clay applied to a standard Bluebird. We were surprised how many man-hours went into this stage as they tweaked subtle details, see pic page 72. Finally they were satisfied though and fibreglass moulds were taken, then six sets of front and rear components made. The new bodywork debuted at the Sandown 400 Endurance Race.

The IHI turbocharger saga

After a year or so of continuously feeding new, $1500 T3 Garrett turbochargers[3] to the cause (original equipment on the Turbo road car) and trying everything we could possibly think of, apart from going slower, to achieve some reliability, (a commentator at the Silastic 300 that year, presumably quoting an informed source, stated that we'd blown up 44 turbochargers to that point in time, although Pete Anderson who'd apparently been keeping score reckoned the total was nearer 100 before we finished – I so wish I'd kept decent records of all this sort of thing.) Howard and Fred put their heads together and decided to explore alternative turbocharger manufacturers.

The Japanese IHI seemed a reasonable possibility and so, Fred tells us but which I doubt, he sent an engine to Japan and IHI spec'd a unit to suit it and subsequently sent us a supply – about six from memory.

I remember a conversation with Howard at Healey Road where, in the context of exploding turbochargers as we strove for performance improvements, I tried to explain what I'd learnt and that what we needed was a turbocharger that could pump a much greater volume of air. He couldn't or wouldn't hear me or didn't understand though – suggesting once again that we instead raise the compression ratio and cut back the boost, which I knew would make less power, and none of us wanted that

---

3   1983 dollars! I only learned the cost recently and was rather shocked. I see you can buy a new standard T3 Garrett turbocharger on eBay for $125 these days!

(although who really knew what Howard wanted).

It was almost always very difficult to know what HM was thinking, having had ample evidence that his actions didn't often match his words, but I felt that he'd begun to give up on me and had probably begun thinking that further development could be done through Sydney. As you'll recall, Fred had begun adding 'development driver' to his credentials and had disseminated this status to the interested media. In retrospect I believe this conversation with Howard was probably another step on the path to Fred taking over the team. As I've said we weren't privy to the inner workings.

So, while we'd been exploring the ragged edge of reliability with boost pressure, and our competitors were receiving more and more concessions, we'd been pressing Howard harder to prosecute our case with CAMS for a relaxation of our turbocharger spec.

Disappointingly though, Howard's claims were either not presented or not given gravitas. Our cars had shown they were capable of competing in the outright class but in truth the engines/turbochargers were being pushed ever harder and the improvements we were making were just not keeping pace with the advances being made by our competitors. As Product Development Manager, Howard would have been keen for the bragging rights of success with a near standard specification engine. Weighing this with the sight of Nissan Bluebirds more and more often expiring in a huge cloud of blue smoke, must however have tormented him. To be continued after the Silastic 300…

1983 AUSTRALIAN ENDURANCE CHAMPIONSHIP

The BB3 build continued apace at Healey Road and we entered the Endurance Championship in 1983 having been pushed up into the over 3-litre class but with no further allowances other than the increase in wheel size, now 16" diameter and wider, that came with our 'promotion'. While we'd battled hard and pushed our equipment past its limits, all our competitors had been given allowances, which it seemed, would take them out of our reach.

The move to the over 3 litre class eventually led to the Bluebirds switching to car numbers 15 and 16, beginning September at Sandown.

For 1983 The Australian Endurance Championship was extended by one round, to include the Silastic 300 at Amaroo, not that anyone outside those competing really knew or much cared. The AEC was never seriously promoted by CAMS or followed by the public as a manufacturers' series. What people cared about was which of their heroes won the James Hardie 1000 at Bathurst and, to a much lesser degree, the Castrol 400 at Sandown. The other races, at Amaroo and Oran Park, were promoted as lead-up races or in the case of Surfers and Adelaide after Bathurst, hardly at all. Still, Howard seemed to think the series was important and that was good enough for us, and for Nissan to keep paying the bills.

AEC Round 1 Silastic 300, Amaroo Park, Sydney, NSW, August 6-7

This would be the first event to expose the results of the freedoms announced during the Oran Park ATCC round in May and there was nervous anticipation in the air as the teams arrived at the dinky circuit.

Surprise, surprise, Terry Shiel with his RX-7 still running a 12A engine, won pole with a 52.1 second lap, Barry Jones' RX-7 which had been updated with a 13B was next fastest with 52.3, then Fury, still running as #55, got to be on the inside of row 2 with a 52.4 and alongside him would be the Grice/Bond STP Commodore. Brock could only manage 52.9 putting him further back on the grid than he'd been in recent years. Finnigan's 53.3 put him alongside Brock on the third row. Freddy Gibson, at his home circuit in the #56 Bluebird could only manage seventh for the inside of row four with Harvey in the second HDT Commodore alongside. Richards in the BMW could do no better than 11th fastest.

Peter McLeod who'd been expected to do well at Amaroo exploded his brand new 13B engine in Friday's practice before he'd had a chance to do a quick lap so, after a fast trip back to Canberra to collect his old 12A and get it bolted in, he was required to start the race from the rear of the grid.

On a warm and cloudless Sunday morning the race burst into action and Jones bolted into the lead by the first turn. By the end of lap 1 though, it was Grice in the lead having gotten past Jones, Shiel and Fury! Had he forgotten this was a 155 lapper? Shiel seemed to be slowing and it became evident his Mazda engine was not well – he retired on lap 12.

McLeod though, driving like a demon, had risen to eighth from the back of the field.

Over Nissan Skyline, Fury hunting down Brock on lap 22.

Fury got past Brock for third place on lap 23 and then two laps later, Grice lapped Gibson. On lap 28, and about to be lapped by Fury on his home circuit, Gibson pitted for an unscheduled stop with what he thought was a boost leak – claimed he had 1.2 bar instead of 1.6 (TV coverage shows myself hunting for a source of a boost leak with Fred's mechanic, Wyn looking on and then Den joined in.) We were unable to find anything to explain low boost and he retired soon after.

On lap 29, second placed Jones' RX-7 pitted with its engine sounding very rough, then Richards passed Harvey into fourth. At lap 36 Fury was second, about three seconds behind Grice and then got past into P1 on about lap 41. Later in that lap Fury also passed Richards' BMW in a great braking dual to lap him.

At 57 laps it was Fury leading Grice, then Brock, Finnigan, McLeod. Fury pitted on lap 64 for fuel and tyres and came out in fourth place but was quickly back to second and retook the lead on lap 78.

Fury, Brock, Richards, McLeod at lap 96. Only Brock was on same lap as Fury but then Brock had his second stop on lap 120 leaving only George on the lead lap.

Last time into Wunderlich Corner, a clear winner.

Final result was Fury first, taking his first touring car win, Brock more than a lap back in second place, and more than two laps further back was McLeod in his RX-7. Of these only George drove the whole race – Brock had shared with Larry Perkins and Peter McLeod with Graham Bailey.

Needless to say, George was the clear leader of the AEC Drivers Championship and Nissan the Manufactures title after the first round.

For the Monday morning after the Silastic 300, Howard and Fred had organised a testing session and I'm told the IHI engineers were in attendance. I don't remember much of this as I was a bit under the weather after a big night celebrating our great win but I'm happy to rely on better memories that mine. I apparently bolted on the first IHI turbocharger, having previously moved the studs in an exhaust manifold to suit the different mounting pattern.

It may have done one hot lap, but not much more, before this too exploded in the, by now very familiar manner – turbine wheel throwing blades immediately followed by wheel breaking off the shaft, all at very high speed and causing catastrophic damage to the turbine housing.

Maybe it was a faulty one, someone thought, so I proceeded to clean up the mess and bolted on a new one. Ditto, another huge cloud of smoke as engine oil under pressure squirted into the hot exhaust[4].

From collective memory that was enough and we packed up. Apparently, when Fred reported our less than stellar results to the IHI higher level, he was told "You should have told us they were intended for racing." Hahaha, nothing like a good belly laugh after a hard day hungover and fingers burned.

IHI must have got back to us with a revised spec unit because I believe Sandown was the first time we ran one in a race. We could really have done without this interlude though – we would have arrived at the much better solution that much sooner.

We completed the build of the third Bluebird Turbo (BB3) and had it sorted in time for it to run at Round 2 of the Endurance Championship at Oran Park. This was to be the last event for the cars running separate bumper bars with rubber insert and ends.

A point of interest is that the roll cage on the new car was welded together in place, which had required the roof to be removed so the tubes could be welded all around. The two earlier cars had bolt together cages and, as already stated, BB1 with components built in Australia and shipped to Japan.

---

4   To be fair, these were new out of the box and had not received the extra fine balancing and tweaking treatment the Garrett turbos were invariably given at that time.

AEC Round 2 Oran Park 250, Sydney, NSW, August 20-21

We went to Oran Park expecting to run all three Bluebirds in the race. It had been decided somewhere in the echelons of Nissan's management that Hasemi and Hoshino wouldn't be coming out for the James Hardie 1000 again so Gary Scott had been recruited to share with George Fury as had John French to partner Fred Gibson. This Oran Park race would be an opportunity to give them both some miles in the cars. That plan looked a bit shaky though when Gary Scott crashed BB2 (#55) early in practice. It was decided that Gibson would stand down for the weekend allowing French to co-drive with Scott. Fury would drive solo in the new car as #57.

Gary keeping an eye on Wyn's tweakings on Sunday morning.

Johnson was easily the fastest qualifier in his newly green-painted Greens' Tuf XE Falcon on 1:14.9, Hansford's Stuyvesant RX-7 (still with a 12A engine) was second fastest with 1:15.5 followed by Fury, third fastest with a 1:15.6. Shiel was next quickest in his RX-7 but didn't take his place at the start on Sunday. Next was Gibson in Bluebird #56 with a 1:15.7, and then Richards in the black BMW 635i with 1:16.2 and McLeod in the Slick 50 RX-7 was alongside Jim.

Johnson had a blinder of a start and headed off into the distance with Fury in his wake and leaving Hansford and the other RX-7s jockeying for position and holding up Gibson. Johnson pulled away with apparent effortless ease – he had the big Falcon handling well at last.

The Mazda drivers had them fully 'wound up' by lap 6 and first Bailey in McLeod's RX-7 then Hansford in one of Moffat's, managed to slip past Fury. At half distance, after Bailey had completed a 50 second scheduled stop, it was Johnson clear to Hansford keeping Fury and Gibson at bay.

Next to the pits was the BMW with a deranged front spoiler and Richards sat there while his team fitted a new one and his position in the race slipped away.

Then Hansford was in for a 15-second fuel stop, which proved to be a mistake for he was back not long after for the tyre change his team should have opted for with the fuel. A further 90-second stop put paid to his chances in the race.

Next was George's stop and we were able to get the tank full and four wheels changed in just 23.5 seconds, so that soon after he resumed the circuit he was second to Johnson and the only other car on the leading lap. Johnson hadn't yet stopped though...

Lap 69 was the turning point in the race as Johnson stormed into the pits and the big green Falcon was in the air, wheel nuts off, and... nothing, the new BBS wheels would not come off their studs! By the time the team had managed to kick them off and get him underway again, Dick was back in fifth place and his race was shot.

George and Gary heading out to the start grid.

On lap 75 the order was George Fury, Terry Finnigan in the Triple M Commodore, Peter McLeod's RX-7, Gary Scott, who'd taken over from Gibson in the second Bluebird and Dick Johnson who was charging hard to make up the deficit. Scott managed to get #56 up to third and it was looking good for a 1-3 for Nissan until the unlucky last of the 100 laps where the turbocharger blew in #56 and Gary limped back to the pits.

Fury had responded to Johnson's late challenge and he ended up winning by some 32 seconds. McLeod came third, Carter fourth and Hansford fifth, all in RX-7s.

Two AEC wins on the trot was a great result for George, our team and for Howard "The Toff" Marsden – so described by the Australian Motor Racing Yearbook correspondent and a name I'd never seen or heard applied to HM before or since, although it wasn't hard to see how some would consider it appropriate.

After two rounds of the 1983 AEC, George was leading the Drivers Table on 50 points, Nissan the Manufacturers Table also on 50 points. Daylight second on both counts.

AEC Round 3 Castrol 400, Sandown Raceway, Victoria, September 10-11

This was a weekend of firsts. The new car's first event running as #15, the debut of the new front and rear fibreglass bodywork and also the first event for car #60, the EXA Turbo, which incidentally was not due for release in Australia for another two weeks.

Pete Anderson confirmed:

"The new Bluebird raced at Oran Park as #57 and then became #15, BB2, up until then raced as #55, became #16 and BB1, the Japanese prepared car, previously raced as #56, became the "T" (test) car. (This is the car I owned for 18 years until a few years ago).

I remember when car #55 changed to #16, Wyn and Trevor added another tube in the roll cage for seat belt attachment behind the driver (Fred's preference to the original setup we had). They'd also done this to Car #56."

The first race meeting where the cars belched flame on gear changes. Not sure why now – possibly a camshaft change.

The second tranche of specification freedoms for 1983 came into effect at Sandown as well. We'd been granted permission to run a supposedly more reliable turbocharger – the IHI. It proved to be less so. According to Will Hagon (commentating) this was the first time we'd run a remotely adjustable wastegate but that wasn't so. It may have been the first time it was easily accessible by the driver but I doubt that too.

Following the highly dangerous situation involving Moffat (and others) speeding in the narrow pit lane and the havoc it caused in the 1982 event, that piece of roadway had been considerably widened which was good although it narrowed pit straight somewhat. The paddock area[5] (behind the pit lane) was however in an atrocious state following recent rain with huge puddles and ankle-deep mud everywhere making things extremely onerous for all. Decidedly not good.

Regarding the very limited amount of practice time here, in an interview Fury told commentator Neil Crompton that *"we are still finding the limit of the new turbocharger and have destroyed a couple in the process."*

---

5   Where cars and transporters were held and work carried out between sessions.

The fastest five cars, Brock, Johnson, Moffat, Richards and Grice, bettered the Touring Car lap record in the second (dry) practice session and the grid for Sunday's race was little changed from this order. Brock then Johnson then Grice all on 1:10.7, Moffat, who was actually fourth fastest on 1:11.2, was moved back to sixth due to a successful protest against his rear wheel widths, so fourth became David Parson's Commodore with 1:11.3, then Fury fifth with a 1:11.4, and Moffat sixth after a small penalty on 1:11.6, Richards seventh with a 1:11.7, Masterton eighth with 1:12.3, McLeod ninth with 1:12.5, and tenth was Gary Rogers with 1:12.6. Fred Gibson was 15th on the grid with a 1:13.5, and Christine Gibson in the EXA Turbo was 25th with a 1:18.7.

All the controversy no doubt served to boost public interest in the race and come Sunday the extensive grandstands and viewing areas were packed. It was a cool and overcast day with rain threatening. Good turbo weather!

Johnson again made a great start and initially looked as though he was going to leave the rest in his dust but by the time they'd arrived at turn 1, Brock had passed and it was clear the green Falcon was in trouble. Up the back straight, with Johnson being passed by half the field, it was Brock then Grice then Fury then Richards, Masterton, Parsons, McLeod, Harvey, Rogers, Moffat and Gibson in 12th. Johnson retired at the end of lap 1 with a failed clutch.

Brock and Grice raced hard and Grice got through to lead on lap 5. Then, on the next, Richards passed Fury and Moffat who'd been carving his way forward also had a go in turn 2 but George kept him out. This proved to be just a delay to the inevitable as Moffat sailed past him next time down the main straight.

On lap 10 Fury suddenly slowed on the back straight and belched the tell-tail cloud of blue smoke from the exhaust telling all that his turbocharger's race was run. He cruised into the pits and turned straight into the paddock to retire.

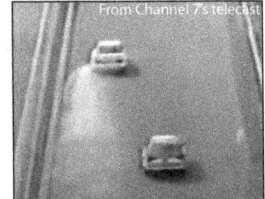
Poof, there goes another IHI.

The TV commentators, agreeing it was a turbo failure, spoke of the IHI turbocharger and of how Marsden had earlier suggested Fred and George would be running different brands (Garrett / IHI) this weekend. When asked about 'the new turbo' by the pit commentator, Howard said that George was not using an IHI but a Garrett, but from both pre-race comments and George's interview soon after, it was very clear that he had the IHI – diplomatic speak I assume to keep the new turbo supplier onside. Interesting that none of the commentators or journos who reported on the race picked up on this anomaly. Or maybe they did but chose not to embarrass Lord Howard.

Three laps later Moffat drove past Brock on the straight and set off after Grice. Christine's EXA Turbo was lapped on about lap 18. Moffat drove past Grice on the back straight on lap 20 and then immediately the STP Commodore's engine seized causing a huge lose off onto the grass. Grice was out. Not what his engine-oil-treatment sponsor wanted to see, I'm sure.

After just 21 laps Moffat had come through from sixth place on the grid to lead the race by almost six seconds to Brock who shortly afterwards lost brakes and hit the wall somewhere on pit straight. It was a glancing blow and he managed to untidily get around the circuit again and back to the pits. Just then John Harvey pitted for a second time with a flat front tyre and pulled #25 right in behind #05. Brock grabbed the opportunity of retiring Harvey instead of himself and soon charged out to rejoin the race in sixth place, two laps adrift.

Fred in #16. Note the very narrow and dangerous pit lane.

Fred came into the pits on lap 22 and HM sent him to the paddock as soon as they'd spoken (I don't remember and haven't been able to discover why). Christine Gibson was leading the 3-litre class by five seconds in the EXA and she completed her scheduled stop on lap 69-ish.

After everyone had completed their fuel and tyre stop, Moffat led by about 30 seconds to Richards followed by two other RX-7s which were at least a lap down. Gary Rogers' Commodore returned to the pits with engine steaming and retired. Christine also returned to pits for an unscheduled stop on about lap 76. There was lots of looking and poking around under the bonnet then the EXA was pushed behind the pits to join its big brothers – the gearbox had failed. What a disappointment after such a good first-up showing for the EXA, Christine, and for our whole team after such a dominant start to the series.

Moffat cruised through most of the event at a leisurely pace, finally winning by 16 seconds to Jim Richards and then Brock (in the second HDT car #25) about two laps behind Richards. Moffat, who'd only been given one churn of fuel since the start and no tyres, slowed considerably in an effort to either finish the race or to engineer a two Stuyvesant RX-7 photo finish but ran out of fuel on the cool down lap before he could get to the presentation area at the start/finish line. Another Sandown shemozzle.

Brock was later disqualified for his mid-race car switch, boosting Jim Richards in the JPS BMW to second, Cullen/Harrop in the K-mart Commodore third and then RX-7s filled seven of the next nine places.

Endurance Championship Drivers' points after Sandown were Fury 50, Richards 43, Moffat 25.

And for the Manufacturers title, Holden 56, Nissan 50, Mazda 40, Ford 37.

AEC Round 4 James Hardie 1000, Bathurst, NSW, October 1-2

Team Accommodation was at The Knickerbocker Hotel initially... Some pre-race memories from the boys. Dave Thompson again:

"I remember that for '83 you or Jamie [probably Ron] had organized alternative accommodation (from the University where we'd stayed the previous year) to one of the Bathurst pubs that you'd booked 12 months in advance for the team."

George Smith chipped in:

"1983 was the year Australia won the Americas Cup. We were initially staying at the Knickerbocker Hotel in the Main Street of Bathurst... we were all in one room watching the deciding race on the telly early in the morning – the lady co-owner of the hotel was walking around drinking Champagne to celebrate!"

Now Pete Anderson:

"...anyway, when Thursday arrived we discovered that the company [Nissan] had commandeered our booking for the Nissan 'Big Wigs' who'd decided to attend at the last minute! So someone from head office had arranged alternative digs for the workers.

It was out of town on a large property that used to run horses, with converted bluestone stables as accommodation. They were to provide us with a meal that evening, however after changing engines in three cars and all the other required preparation for the race on Sunday we arrived at about 8:30pm and we were promptly told that dinner finished at 8:00 and we'd missed out!

We then inspected the accommodation – cold rooms no heating and not much better than sacks for beds! We were to say the least, unimpressed with this whole episode so we returned to the Bathurst township, had dinner at The Stagecoach and searched the town for any sleeping bags/bedding we could find so we could sleep in the heated Pantech on the benches!"

Back to George again:

"Correct! I remember Ronny Motorsport in the BoyBus with us driving around looking for a camping store to buy blankets, sleeping bags etc. whatever... he was worried what the cost was going to run up to.

In the end it was 'Marquee Mal'[6] to the rescue as he had a store

---

6 'Marquee Mal' was a contractor Nissan used for corporate events. He'd bring

of blankets he used to wrap up goods for transporting.

After that we returned to a hotel bar to have a drink or three. I remember Ronny Motorsport was in charge of the cash, when we needed more money Ronny would hand some over as requested.

Den asked for $20 and Ronny handed it over. Then Den, being a smoker, pulled out his lighter, lit the 20 and then lit his cigarette from it, then dropped the burning 20 in the ash trough at the front of the bar.

Ronny was very reluctant to hand over the $50 that was requested next, fearing its imminent demise – such a funny time!!"

Now stop chuckling 'cos it's about to get serious again.

Yes, at Mt Panorama in particular, car racing can be a very dangerous sport!

The 1983 Hardies Heroes (now just a single flying lap timed to a hundreth of a second) was notable for Dick Johnson's horrific crash coming out of Forest's Elbow. Exiting onto Conrod Straight the rear of the car touched the Armco barrier which pulled the front of the car around into the end of the barrier causing it to head off the track and into a treed gully. Brock was next car along on his warm-up lap and stopped to check on Johnson. He gave a very shaken but otherwise unharmed DJ a lift back to the pits before restarting his own run.

Fury had qualified second fastest with a 2:17.2 and was also second in Hardies Heroes with a slightly slower 2:17.509 – fastest to that point in the top ten run-off. Richards' BMW ran next and did a 2:18.414. Then Brock somewhat spoiled our morning with a 2:16.270.

There is a terrific story of the 1983 Bathurst week by Phil Scott for Wheels Magazine at https://www.whichcar.com.au/features/39-years-of-holden-commodore/1983-holden-commodore-boos-blues-and-brock so I won't give you a blow-by-blow here. The following is mostly just the

---

and erect marquees etc. at the race tracks and was a very handy guy to have at our disposal. Mal arranged manufacture of our own marquee that attached to the side of our Pantech but before that he'd hire Nissan a tent for our use at meetings.

Brock amused us briefly on the grid with his Ben Lexcen approved 'secret winged keel'.

story as it affected our team.

So the grid for race-day was Brock/Perkins on pole, Fury/Scott (the first non V8 car to start from the front row since 1973, when Brock qualified second fastest in his Torana XU-1), Parsons/Janson, Richards/Gardner, Harvey/Brock, Cullen/Harrop, Rogers/Benson-Brown, Grice/Bond, Morris/Rusty French and then Johnson/Bartlett in a borrowed XE Falcon after his huge crash. Moffat could mysteriously only manage 14th place with his RX-7 that had so easily dominated Sandown just three weeks earlier, two places behind Hansford whose Stuyvesant RX-7 was still running a 12A. There was a fresh round of allegations of foxing doing the rounds of the paddock. Fred Gibson qualified #16 in 18th position.

Christine Gibson in the #60 EXA Turbo blitzed the 3-litre class by just over three seconds in qualifying with a 2:27.1 to place herself and Bob Muir 37th on the grid.

The Stuyvesant team had their huge, all enclosed, blue and white annex attached to the side of their transporter and at Bathurst in '83 this was a no-go area for anyone other than card-carrying team members. This was vigorously enforced by pistol-toting security guards! It became known as the Canvas Vatican and Moffat named Pope Allan. The usual camaraderie and socialising between teams at Mt Panorama that year, and indeed from then on, did not include team Stuyvesant, all of this doing nothing to ease the rumours of cheating and foxing. Even though Moffat had qualified a lowly 14th it was he the media flocked around and wanted to hear from – Bob Morris' heroic effort in making it into the top 10 shoot out, and Fury's also heroic efforts in getting the Bluebird onto the front row was largely ignored. Pope Allan must have been chuckling inside the Canvas Vatican.

The big race itself was notable for being the first to be won by three drivers – Brock again needing two cars to get the job done. Following his disqualification from the Sandown 400 results, for this race the four HDT drivers had been cross-nominated for cars #05 and #25.

Johnson's team had overnight performed a near miracle to get what was left of his #17 Green's Tuff Falcon into another Falcon race car that was offered to him. They even painted it green, had it sign written and got it to the grid in time for the start. Amusingly, commentator Evan Green got green paint on the sleeves of his lovely red Channel 7 jacket as he leaned in to chat with Dick on the start line – getting the car ready for the race must have been a very close thing. Not long into the race however, it was having battery charging problems and it was in and out of the pits.

The race began well for most and Brock narrowly led Fury into Hell Corner followed by Harvey, Parsons, Richards' BMW then a hoard of Commodores and a few Falcons. Gibson passed three cars on the drag to turn 1. While holding a strong second place, Fury's

Thousands of horsepower unleashed an' heading to Hell.

Bluebird slowed dramatically on pit straight at the end of lap 1 and George did a slow lap without 2nd and 3rd gears to get back to the pits. It took our team 13 laps (approx. 30 minutes) to change the gearbox (not bad on a hot racecar without a hoist) and then #15 was out again, circulating rapidly albeit with hopes for success severely diminished.

Richard's BMW slowed and also went to the pits at the end of lap 2 and then, on lap 8, Brock's 05 Commodore broke a connecting rod (on Conrod straight would you believe!) and smokily limped into the pits to retire. The BMW was in and out of the pits for several laps with what they discovered to be ground up aluminium in the fuel, clogging the injectors. A commentator suggested sabotage but team boss Frank Gardner was disinclined to agree. I reckon they likely had a fuel pump eating itself. They gave up after a few more laps, apparently unable to resolve the problem in any sort of reasonable time frame.

As they say, you can't please all the people all of the time!

Of the fancied contenders still running on lap 14, only Grice, Harvey and Moffat remained in contention. I'm sure Brock didn't expect his cunning backup plan to be needed so early but on lap 20 Harvey was brought in for an early fuel and tyre stop and it was Brock who roared back into the race in car #25. The EXA also exited the race on lap 14 with a blown head gasket. In an interview with Peter Wherrett, Christine talked about how difficult the car was to drive due to torque-steer although praised its handling and performance – it had been lapping 3 seconds a lap faster than any other 3-litre car.

Meanwhile, driving steadily and helped by the extreme mortality among the top runners, Gibson managed to get #16 up to sixth place at around the 30 lap mark. Allan Grice, who'd gotten past Brock on lap 5, held onto the lead through to his first stop on lap 38 where he handed over to Colin Bond during a somewhat tardy, one-minute pit stop.

With all the V8s needing to stop for fuel, Moffat cruised into the lead on lap 40 but then, even though a tyre change wasn't required, car #43 had a rather long and chaotic stop as they switched drivers and then Katayama, after not being able to select a gear, finally resumed in third place behind Grice and Brock.

After all this drama in the first third, the race turned comparatively dull. For Team Nissan our interest was maintained via a TV monitor in our pit. George's was one of the few cars carrying RaceCam for the telecast so the director was often switching back to the car #15 camera, allowing us to see Fury reeling in V8s and hear him cussing them if they didn't immediately give way to his passing attempts! It would have been good to hear or see his lap times – race coverage has certainly come a long way since 1983.

Racecam could show the view through windscreen, pivot to spy on the driver or show the view behind. It was a popular alternative camera platform for the telecast director. We were able to follow our gun car's progress and often see Fury and then Scott circulating at or around the leaders' pace, at one stage racing hard with, and then passing Moffat's co-driver Katayama.

Going in to the second half of the race, Perkins/Brock/Harvey were in the lead with Katayama/Moffat second and Grice/Bond in third, the only cars on the same lap.

Mid afternoon somewhere the #15 Bluebird was back in the pits with a boost leak from the compressor to intercooler pipe. We were able to

THE STORY – 1983

Nissan's Mt Panorama hospitality area alongside Conrod Straight, thanks to Marquee Mal, ready to entertain. There on the left is the racecar mock-up, we built from a Diesel model Bluebird and which is still on display at the Bathurst Museum, although I believe it has been subsequently fitted with a turbo petrol engine.

George exiting Murray's Corner onto Pit Straight about to start his hot lap for Hardies Heroes.

Assembled on the start grid, no doubt with butterflies swirling.

Brock narrowly leads Fury in the race to turn 1, shortly after the flag fell to start the 1983 'Great Race'.

Fred hard at work heading down through the Esses.

Christine guides the EXA down to Forrest's Elbow while giving the heavyweights plenty of room to dance. The Gregorys sign is pointing vaguely toward the newsagent in the Bathurst township in case you're wondering.

Fury's Bluebird getting a little air going over the top at Skyline.

Gary rapidly losing altitude, charging down into Forest's Elbow.

overcome this in short order and Scott was again out passing V8s – in fact at one stage the commentator announced that our Bluebird was the fastest car on the track – we saw it pass and go away from Perkins who was leading the race at that time. French/Gibson were still going, at that time in eighth place, a lap down on the leaders while Scott/Fury were down twelve laps in 29th place.

At about lap 120 the French/Gibson turbocharger cried enough and car #16 came into the pits belching copious amounts of blue smoke. They lost 8 or so laps while we changed the turbo and Fred was out circulating again in approximately 20th place.

Other than a good dice between Brock and Moffat for about 10 laps, albeit with Moffat a lap behind, the race turned into a procession as it usually does, with the top 10 drivers separated by minutes or laps. With just 20 laps remaining, after some 10 laps pursuing Moffat's RX-7, #55 was in the pits again with gearbox trouble. It was decided to call it a day.

The final results were Brock/Harvey/Perkins' #25 Commodore first with 163 laps – the first time three drivers had shared a wining car at Bathurst, although the strategy was largely not appreciated by race fans and the win was probably his least popular. For the second race in a row Phil Brock (co-driver for #25) missed out on even sitting in the car.

This must have been pre-race :-)

Moffat/Katayama played tortoise but were uncharacteristically let down by poor pit work, not helped by a driver's door that could not be opened from early in the race. The Stuyvesant RX-7 finished second, one lap down. The Grice/Bond STP Roadways Commodore was third with 160 laps and then their second team car driven by Harrington/Wigston, fourth with 158 laps. Close behind in fifth was McLeod/Bailey's RX-7. The Gibson/French Bluebird #16 placed 22nd with 134 laps. It would be Fred Gibson's last event as a Nissan driver. Fury/Scott scored a DNF although they were credited with 130 laps completed and raced hard following the gearbox change, claiming back several of the laps they'd lost.

Regarding the hot rumours, at and following Bathurst, that Moffat had used a 6-speed gearbox in the RX-7, in a years-later televised chat between Brock and Harvey, Brock was still being very careful to say 'allegedly' when Harvey brought up the subject. Bazza Bray relates the tale of bumping into Mike Webb (Moffat's chief mechanic) coming out of Hollinger Engineering carrying a 6-speed gearbox at about this time.

The record shows that the Holden Dealer Team Commodores were the dominant force at this, Australia's toughest test for touring cars of the era. They were built capable of running near their top speed all day and their team would reliably get their scheduled pit stops done in half the time taken by other V8 teams. An engine blow-up was a small blip on the record of what they were able to achieve. The Bathurst 1000 at this time was still a race for big V8s with carburettors but the cracks were starting to show.

Endurance Championship Drivers' points after Bathurst were Fury 50, Moffat 48, Richards 43, McLeod 35.

And for the Manufacturers title, Holden 81, Mazda 65, Ford 61, Nissan 50, BMW 43.

When George Smith dismantled the gearboxes that had let us down he discovered that the mainshaft drive for second and third gears had failed – one of the three ears that drive the gear-coupling ring had sheared off – a repeat of the failure at the 1982 Adelaide Touring Car Championship round and, I assume, the Hasemi/Hoshino car at the '81 James Hardie 1000, although we Aussies didn't get to see the inside of that gearbox. George set about designing replacement dog-meshing gears, drives and shafts for second through fifth gears and then he and Howard went off to consult with Peter Hollinger.

The wait for these components to be made and the subsequent building of the resulting bulletproof gearboxes among other projects caused us to miss the trip to Surfers Paradise for the final AEC round.

We took BB#1 to Bathurst as a test/comparison car.

AEC Round 5 Surfers Paradise Raceway, Gold Coast, Qld, October 29-30

Only the EXA travelled to Surfers for this meeting. Back at the workshop the best idea we could come up with to address the head gasket failure was a solid copper gasket with combustion chamber sealing rings but though this was an improvement, the Surfers round would only help cement the EXA Turbo's reputation as a 'fast but fragile little weapon' – it again blitzed the under 3-litre class in qualifying with a 1:18.7, almost three seconds faster than Glen Seton's 1:21.4 in his Ford Capri V6.

Christine cleared off from her class competitors at the start of the 95-lap race but came back to the field at about the 40-lap mark when she slowed due to an overheating engine but soldiered on. At lap 55 she brought it in for fuel and tyres and 15 laps later was back with a badly misfiring engine. Spark plugs were examined but compression was low and it could not be coaxed into restarting, the overheating had compromised the head gasket seal.

Meanwhile Brock, who'd started on pole, charged away from a pack of Commodores that included Grice and Finnigan and looked like he'd cleanup once again until on lap 35 when #05 pulled off the track in a cloud of smoke, this time from the differential. With no second HDT car in the race Brock was left high and dry and was relegated to spectator status.

Second-place-man Grice inherited the lead and this time had some luck and held on to take the race. Dick Johnson (Falcon), Terry Finnigan, Gary Rodgers, Geoff Russell, Barry Lawrence (Commodores), Jim Richards (BMW) and Gregg Hansford, Terry Shiel and Peter McLeod (Mazda RX-7s) battled for the minor placings and, in the end, Hansford placed second on the same lap as Grice, McLeod third, and Finnigan fourth, both a lap behind, and Lawrence fifth, two laps back. Seton placed 10th in the Capri completing 88 laps and dominating the 3-litre class. Once again the attrition was higher than the spectators would have preferred.

To finish first, first you must finish. Looking good until lap 40...

1983 Australian Grand Prix, Berri Fruit Juice Touring Car Trophy support race at Calder Motor Raceway, November 12-13

One week before the scheduled final round of the AEC there was a well-supported Touring Car support race to the Australian Grand Prix on the calendar at Calder Park and due to our sorry position in the AEC standings, the comparative media interest and no doubt Calder's proximity to our base, it was decided we'd put our remaining energy and budget toward this meeting in preference to the last AEC round in Adelaide.

Howard had been in Japan and had arranged to fly in and come straight to the track from the airport to join us mid way through Saturday practice.

We'd begun practice and George had already done some quick laps under the watching eye of relief team manager Fred Gibson. I can't clearly remember now why we took the Bluebird to Calder with a 2.2-litre (Z22) engine under the bonnet and those of us remaining don't completely agree on our motivation for doing so but I do feel sure it was tied in with our exasperation at seeing our hard won competitiveness badly eroded by the spec. freedoms allowed to our competitors and our boss's failure to fight our cause.

We must have thought, what the hell, it's the last race for the season, it isn't part of a series, let's show 'em what's possible…, or something similar.

Anyway, George, in blissful ignorance, had done a few laps faster than any we'd done out there before – and then a travel fatigued Howard arrived.

When Fred tipped him off about what was afoot HM absolutely blew his stack, something none of us had ever witnessed before – in my own case in nine years of working with him, often under pressure. What all surviving witnesses clearly remember is Howard literally shaking and his voice quivering – he demanded we all assemble in the transporter.

Fred was last in and Howard asked him to close the door. He joined Howard, maybe to support him if he went weak in the knees. It went something like: *"What on earth were you thinking? Get that engine out and a legal one in there before I change my mind and sack you all! We'll be talking further about this in my office on Monday morning!"* Then he and Fred stormed off and left us to it.

Long international flights will do that to even the most mild-mannered of us. It was interesting to see that aspect of him exposed, not that any of us was thinking that at the time.

Anyway, we whipped the Z22 engine out and slotted in the Z18 we'd brought as a spare, then Bazza and I high-tailed it back to the workshop to get started on a fix for the EXA head gasket and the rest of the team climbed aboard the Nissan Vanette, our troop carrier at the time, and speared off to the Keilor Pub to salve their woes.

According to Fred's account of this episode in a 2013 article published on SpeedCafe.com, he said *"I've never seen Howard so annoyed, he was shaking. They had a meeting in his office on Monday morning and I think he sacked three guys."*

Well, that's not quite what occurred, not only was no one sacked but Howard was nowhere to be found on Monday morning – we'd asked Ronnie to call his secretary to set up a meeting but she'd no idea where he was. I can't recall when it was we next saw Howard but we all agree we never heard a single further word on the subject.

Somewhat embarrassingly, George Fury told this story to the assembled throng at Howard's very well attended memorial service at the Sofitel Hotel in Collins Street, Melbourne in August 2003.

For the record, the AGP that year was won by Roberto Moreno in a Ralt RT4. Second was a John Smith, third was Jacques Laffite, fourth was Geoff Brabham and fifth, also setting the fastest lap in the race, was Alan Jones!

Following that though was a 40-lap race for tourers with a compulsory pitstop where two tyres were required to be changed. Each car had to stop on a nominated lap – the idea to enhance the spectacle for viewers while avoiding chaos in the pits. George lined up in pole position, having clocked a pretty impressive 44.73 on the Saturday. Brock's best of 44.9 had him next to George on the front row.

Brock got the jump on George when the flag fell and led into turn 1 for the first time with George chewing at his rear bumper. There followed ten laps of extremely hard fought racing until George found a way past, under brakes at the end of the back straight.

Christine also started in this race with the EXA but again suffered overheating (not helped by it being a very hot day) and retired on lap 9. It was never seen on the Channel 7 telecast.

On lap 15 Fury led with Brock less than half a second behind. Perkins was third, back a further 11 seconds, followed by Richards 5 seconds behind Perkins and then Cullen less than a second adrift of the BMW.

Perkins was first of the leaders to make his pitstop and the MHDT team had the car stationary for 18.7 seconds. Fury was next and we had him stopped for 16.6 seconds. Brock's stop took 19.3 seconds, Warren Cullen's guys blotted the copy book with a 36.0 second stop and Jim Richards was also fairly disappointing with a 21.7 second stop, despite the single centre-lock wheel nuts the BMW used.

A pretty slick pitstop slightly increased George's lead.

All this extended George's lead by a little less than three seconds so he was able to cruise to the finish beating Brock by approx. 2.5 seconds and Warren Cullen's Commodore by most of a lap. Perkins had disappeared sometime after his pitstop.

It was great to have been able to win our last race of the year and looking back, better to have won it with a legal setup. But sheesh, what was all the drama for?

At the presentation George was presented with a large trophy, two-litres of Berri orange juice plus a Berri hamper of goods. He said Calder was our team's home circuit and that the car is quick and likes it there.

Then Mr Dunlop presented him with a trophy for being the best-placed car on Dunlops. George said *"thanks, Dunlop has some competition now but they're still the best."*

"Don't go away, don't go away, we haven't finished yet, cos Keith Marshall is here from John Sands", said Gary Wilkinson, and George was presented with a laptop computer, *"to help with your lap scoring"*.

Wilkinson quipped that, *"with all this loot, I wonder if the boot on Howard Marsden's Nissan Bluebird is big enough to carry it all."* To which George replied, *"it already has two computers in it!"*

All smiles and laughs to finish our last race for the year.

AEC Round 6 Adelaide Raceway, South Australia, November 21-20

We didn't have an entry in this race so it holds only academic interest for us but, for the record, Brock started from pole which he'd easily captured in the first practice session among a badly depleted field. Barry Jones' Mazda RX-7 was alongside him and Masterton's Falcon completed the front row on Adelaide's very wide and long straight. Next were Richards' BMW and Cullen's Commodore. The drag down the long straight to turn 1 showed promise for an exciting race but by the end of the lap Brock had already opened a big lead.

For the next seven or eight laps, second placed Richards was holding up a gaggle of cars but then Masterton got through as soon as the BMW's tyres had passed their best. Richards struggled on using three or four sets of fronts for the race.

At 65 laps as the pit stops began, Brock had almost a lap on second placed Barry Jones' RX-7 and he was followed by Steve Masterton's Falcon, Warren Cullen's and Andrew Harris' Commodores, then Peter McLeod's RX-7, all a lap down.

At Brock's stop they refuelled and changed the two outside wheels in a shade over 29 seconds which seems an eternity in this age of sub two second f1 pit stops but it was quick enough to extend his lead by 10 seconds over second place.

Late in the race Masterton's engine blew which elevated Cullen to second, Jones to third, McLeod to fourth and that's how it finished. Brock conducted a master class albeit with no top-level opposition, winning by something more than two laps.

Peter McLeod, coming fourth without having stopped in the race, did enough to win the Driver's Endurance Championship with 72 points. Richards came second in the series with 67, gaining points in all rounds except Bathurst. Fury placed third with 50 points and Moffat fourth with 48 points.

Nissan's great start in the Endurance Championship for Makes was in the end swamped by both Holden and Mazda who jointly won the title with 131 points each. Ford placed third with 84 points and even BMW, who ran only the one car in the series, out-scored us with 67 points – a big disappointment for our team as well as its financier and supporters.

Peter Brock won the Endurance Drivers award with 72 points to Jim

Richards with 67 and George Fury was third with 50, at least beating the two Alans, Moffat with 48 and Grice with 45.

The Z22 engine was taken to Sydney at HM's direction and, I'm led to believe, used by Gary Scott in the #16 Bluebird for the 1984 AMSCAR series.

Gary Scott managed two 2nd places out of the 3 heats in round one of the 1984 AMSCAR series ar Amaroo Park.

Nissan team garb for 1984

1984

As we grew more and more frustrated with CAMS' apparent refusal to allow us a larger turbocharger, further freedom of specs were being handed out almost willy-nilly to our competitors. Around our morning tea table at least, responsibility for this was alternatingly attributed to CAMS and to our leader. Why, we repeatedly questioned, were we not permitted to play on a level playing field.

Moffat for instance, running a sports car in touring car racing, not only had the freedom to use a LHD or RHD car depending on what best suited each track, but also the use of a huge rear wing and guard flares on his Mazda RX7, and we had anecdotal evidence he was running a 6-speed custom gearbox that was clearly outside the rules, not to mention his recently granted allowance to use the larger 13B peripheral-ported, and fuel injected, rotary engine.

Holden and Ford were now permitted to run much larger wheels and tyres – commensurate with their vehicles' weight plus various engine mods such as custom inlet manifolds and modified, larger valved cylinder heads etc. Howard continued to fob us off in his most polite and sympathetic way. I got better and better at changing red-hot hardware in a timely manner, and the closer we got to putting pressure on the front runners the harder it became to back off the boost pressure...

We were also very concerned about the amount of our resources that had been transferred to the Gibson workshop in Sydney, not the least of which was the #56 Bluebird Turbo race-car. There was apparently a plan afoot to which the crew were not privy.

At least we had the two Australian-built Bluebirds at our workshop for 1984. The original Japanese car, despite inspiring us with its early speed in the hands of Hasemi and Hoshino, had later been the least loved and we put it out of mind.

We were unwilling to let all our huge striving go down the drain, and over morning coffee we hatched a plan to approach Jack Wrigley, Nissan's General Manager and Howard's boss, to let him know what was going on. The team-mates had their say and it was decided that I, as the longest serving, and maybe the most diplomatic of us, should be the one to carry our grievances down the road to Head Office.

Probably shaking with apprehension I seem to have totally wiped this episode from my memory so I've had to rely initially on Jamie and then on Bazza and Pete, who both seem to have memories like titanium traps. Wrigley apparently said that he really couldn't challenge Howard without evidence, but from then on he was going to try and get copies of any invoices relating to Fred Gibson and the NSW operation and keep an eye on things that way.

Well, we'd been heard and had let off some steam. It was probably enough for us to get back to work and thinking about how to make the Bluebird go faster and get the turbos not to explode. Nothing further on the matter reached our ears.

I do clearly remember another episode from around this time.

Howard was at the workshop one morning and we were sitting around our morning tea table trying to swallow whatever it was he was telling us and I'd suddenly had enough. I got up when I thought things were winding down and stalked off next door to where I was doing some maintenance work on our Urvan on the hoist.

Howard approached and calmly asked me if I was OK. I told him I was just tired, when what I really meant was I was tired of the BS. I had the Urvan's engine pipe in hand and turned away to refit it, slightly brushing his shirt-sleeve. I apologised, to which he responded, *"It's OK, it wouldn't have been the first black mark you've given me."* I ignored this, not willing to go there, and went about the job. He lingered a while and then walked away.

I've pondered this several times over the years and come up with a few possible explanations for the 'black mark' comment. I think the most likely explanation though, related to my trip to head office to complain to Jack Wrigley. Similar to myself I suppose, Howard had a strong aversion to confrontation – he needed to be seriously rattled before he'd raise his voice or even verbally challenge.

It wasn't long after this though, that Wyn came down from Sydney and left driving our prized 3-litre, triple-Webered, 5-speed Urvan.

1984 AMSCAR Better Brakes Series, Amaroo Park

Once again I'll get the somewhat lack-lustre AMSCAR Series out of the way before we get into the more interesting Touring Car Championship.

The format for this year was once again practice and qualifying on the Saturday to determine the grid positions for the three short races on Sunday – this time five, eight and ten laps.

There was a rather meagre field of just 16 cars in attendance with most of the big names concentrating on the Touring Car Championship.

Fred Gibson had retired from driving after the '83 James Hardy 1000 so the Bluebird #1 was taken over by Gary Scott running with door #16. He managed a few podium finishes and claimed fourth for this series but it was comprehensively won by one of the dinosaurs – Steve Masterton in his XE Falcon.

Christine Gibson drove the EXA Turbo in the first three rounds but it's best result was an outright seventh[1], failing to finish more often than not and crashing out twice, although not of her own making.

AMSCAR Round 1, March 4

Masterton dominated practice with a 52.4 second lap and Scott managed a 53.1 to get along side him on the front row. Christine's best was 54.6 seconds placing her well back on the grid.

In the 5-lapper Scott led away from the start but before the end of the lap Masterton was passing and they touched, causing the Bluebird to spin off and go from first to last. Masterton had an easy win and the EXA placed eighth.

The 8-lapper had a similar start but this time Masterton got past Scott without touching and that was how the race finished – Masterton two seconds to Scott and all the race interest and TV coverage was in the rest of the field, half a lap behind. Christine placed ninth.

Gary 1st and Christine 7th, both off to a good start in heat 1.

---

1 it doesn't appear as though there was an under 3.0 litre class in this series for 1984.

The 10-lapper was a carbon copy of the 8-lapper but with two more laps. The crowd had lost interest but the EXA did a little better to come home seventh.

At least it had been a fine and warm weekend.

AMSCAR Round 2, April 8

Only 14 cars turned up for Round 2 and under clear skies Gary got the bit between his teeth and did an exceptional 51.9 for pole position.

Masterton did a 52.1 for second spot and Christine did a 54.3 for ninth on the start grid.

Sunday's races were run in the spectrum of damp to wet which made it all a bit more exciting for the crowd. Heat one began with Masterton beating Gary to the drop and beating him to the top of the hill. Finnigan was on the charge and nudged the Bluebird in the rear, sending it spinning off – second to last once again! He had the ignominy of following the EXA home in eighth place.

Scott did much better in a very wet Round 2.

...but Mrs Gibson not so well.

In Heat two it was Gary's turn to get the jump on Masterton and they raced together nose to tail for the eight laps. Christine got caught up in a skirmish on lap 1 though and managed to get swatted off the track, finishing up stuck on an earth bank, pointing the wrong way with the little EXA's tail in the air.

Heat three proved to be a reversal of heat two, albeit the EXA a scratching. Masterton's Falcon this time got the jump and Gary's Bluebird bogged down, even letting Richards' BMW into the limelight for three laps until Gary managed to get past.

So, a first, a second and an eighth for Scott in Round two.

AMSCAR Round 3, May 20

15 cars turned up to practice for Round 3 which was dominated by Bob Morris in his green and white State Building Society RX-7 with a best of 51.9, matching Scott's pole time in Round 2. Scott was relegated to second, being able only to do a 52.3 this time and Masterton to third with a 52.5. Christine could only do a 54.3 to put the EXA in 11th place on the grid.

The 5-lap Heat 1 ran as per qualifying, Morris, Scott, Masterton but there was some mayhem back in the field on lap one with one of the Commodores being punted into the earth bank at The Loop, rolling along it and falling back on the track on its roof and remaining there for the rest of the heat. An RX-7 was also involved in the fray and was unable to continue.

Only 12 cars were able to front up for Heat 2 but it was a clone of Heat 1 and Morris led home Masterton followed by Scott.

Morris once again led Heat 3 from start to finish and it looked as though Masterton and Scott would play their parts until Scott had a moment at The Loop in lap one and yet again dropped back to last. The EXA then had a coming together with Burgmann's RX-7 and neither could continue. Gary was working his way back into the placings when the Bluebird had another dreaded turbo detonation.

Ho hum, rather a dreary day.

AMSCAR Round 4, July 8.

Again just 12 cars arrived to practice for the final round of the series. Notable absences were a P. Brock who had apparently entered but did not show, Bob Morris who'd blitzed Round 3 but had subsequently lost his sponsorship, and Christine Gibson whose battered EXA wasn't up for another pummelling. Masterton had pretty much sewn up the series so I guess it wasn't too surprising that many decided not to subject themselves further to this house of pain.

5th, 2nd and 1st in the three heats in Rnd 4. Improving!

Anyway, just for the record, Masterton won pole with a 52.3 followed by Scott, Richards and Finnigan within four tenths.

For the first heat Scott botched the start again and dropped to sixth letting Masterton blast off to a clear lead. Richards and Finnigan battled for the other podium places while Gary battled hard with Burgmann but couldn't find a way past. Masterton's win made his series win beyond doubt and the rest probably wondered why they'd come. Scott got fifth.

Heat 2 was a procession with Masterton leading home Scott followed by Finnigan, Richards and Burgmann.

Scott made a great start in the 10-lap final heat for the series as did Finnigan and they raced nose to tail for the full race providing good entertainment. Masterton cruised to third holding back a slightly frustrated Richards.

Final points for the series were Masterton 112, Finnigan 85, Richards 82, Scott 81 and Wilmington 59.

OK, time to pay attention again.

1984 AUSTRALIAN TOURING CAR CHAMPIONSHIP

Points were awarded for this year's championship as follows:

O/R Placing	1st	2nd	3rd	4th	5th	6th	7th	8th	9th	10th	11th	12th etc
If <3001cc	30	27	24	21	19	17	15	14	13	12	10	9 etc
If >3000cc	25	23	20	17	15	13	11	10	9	8	7	6 etc

ATCC Round 1 Sandown Raceway, Melbourne, Victoria – February 17-18

The lead-up to the opening round of the series had seen speculation swirling – everyone having their say about the relative merits and otherwise of the top contenders. Brock, who could never be discounted at Sandown, silenced the crowd though when he smartly trotted out a pole-winning 1:10.5, three tenths faster than both Moffat's lap record and Johnson's best effort of 1:10.8, Moffat claimed third and completed the front row of the grid with 1:11.1, Masterton fourth, on the second row with 1:11.2, Fury fifth with 1:11.6 and Richards sixth with 1:11.8.

As was to be expected for Melbourne in February it was a hot weekend and it was clear quite early that the Bluebird had slipped back a little in the pack. It was at this meeting where British tyre manufacturer Avon

THE STORY – 1984

Exiting ARCO onto the back straight George is pushed wide by a back marker, but shows he's still got it in the dirt!

began its assault on the Australian Touring Car scene with its radial-ply tyres– users for this race were Moffat, McLeod, Grice and Fury. We'd spent quite some time at Calder getting the suspension tuned for these[2].

On Sunday Brock made a great start and once again sprinted off to take a very solid lead that he masterfully hung onto for the race. Johnson also raced on his own, 6-10 seconds behind. There were several retirements including Grice who went straight on into the tyres at the end of pit straight and then, after Steve Masterton's Falcon retired midway, Moffat also had a lonely race. Then there was a further approximately 10 second gap back to Jim Richards and George Fury who diced the whole race, providing most of the interest, alternatingly sharing fourth and fifth.

Watching the video, it appeared that George had to really fight to get past the BMW but that Richards had a reserve and was able to drive past the Bluebird on the back straight when it suited him. In an interview sometime after the race though, George explained that we'd discovered the turbine wheel in his turbocharger had been intermittently rubbing on its housing thereby slowing its speed and reducing the boost pressure. He sometimes had full power, sometimes not. Presumably it was these times when Richards was able to easily pass. Fury persisted and did well under the circumstances to place fifth. See my notes on turbocharger development from page 169 for further explanation of this.

Brock won with a margin of 13.8 seconds to Johnson and with a further 15.4 seconds to Moffat. Richards came fourth and Fury fifth.

Points score for the ATCC Driver's Championship after Sandown: Brock 25, Johnson 23, Moffat 20, Richards 17 and Fury 15.

---

2   Radial-ply tyres require considerably more negative camber than the cross-plies.

ATCC Round 2 Symmons Plains Raceway, Launceston, Tas. March 10-11

We loaded up early and took both #2 and #3 Bluebirds in the transporter across Bass Straight to Tasmania on the ferry to start practice on the Wednesday. George drove both extensively trying to work up a handling package he was happy with for the race. After having done 150 laps and achieved a reasonably good qualifying time, on the Saturday afternoon the newer car developed an engine miss that we weren't able to find the cause of so in the end we chose to swap doors and bonnets and run the older car in the race as #15.

Moffat had also arrived early with his LHD car and finally managed to snatch pole position with a 58:23. Brock after just a few laps won second spot on 58:54, Johnson got third with a 58:58, Fury was fourth fastest with 58:63 and Richards fifth on 58:73.

This was about as far as Fury got after a drive shaft broke.

Race day was a very cold wintery Tasmanian day and Moffat had brought a nose cover for the RX-7 to keep his engine warm on the grid prior to the start. This backfired badly though as the car overheated causing its engine to fail just after the start. It proved to be a bad day for the Japanese marques, the Bluebird snapped a rear half shaft and moved only about five metres.

All had been for nothing… *"I'm very disappointed. It was a very fraught week and it's ended up quite badly,"* George said in an interview.

Brock took the lead into turn 1 followed by Johnson in his new Greens-Tuf XE Falcon and Grice in a rented SAAS Commodore. Brock worked up a five second lead and hung onto it. Richards' BMW retired just before half distance. The race finished with Brock about 20 seconds ahead of Johnson then about 30 seconds to Grice – ho hum, boring unless you happened to be a V8 fancier.

Points score for the ATCC Driver's Championship after Symmons Plains: Brock 50, Johnson 46, Moffat 20, Grice 20, Richards 17, McLeod 17 and Fury 15

ATCC Round 3. Wanneroo Park, Perth, Western Australia, May 31-April 1

Den and George took the transporter across the Nullarbor to Perth and the rest of the team arrived courtesy of Ansett Airlines. I think here, more than any previous race, I arrived at the track with trepidation at the prospect of failed turbochargers. We'd been left behind in the horsepower stakes and with George then more than happy with the car's handling, cranking up the boost seemed the only tactic left to us.

Moffat, who'd won the 1983 race, set a scorching pace from the first practice session where he quickly put in a 61.76, which wasn't bettered for the rest of the day. Brock didn't muck about either, recording a 62.09 to Fury's 62.34, which George later improved on to grab a front row spot on the grid but exploded a turbocharger trying to further improve on the following lap. Johnson took third grid position with a 62.78 and McLeod did a 62.79 to be fourth.

Fury pulled off into his own smoke at the end of lap 12.

With a smaller than usual field due to the distance most had to do to get there, the race began on a warm and sunny Sunday and it was Moffat, Fury, Brock and Johnson off the line. George started well and was into turn 1 alongside Moffat. Richards retired the BMW on lap 4 but rejoined after time in pits. Moffat – Fury – Brock until lap 13 when Fury's turbocharger failed and he exited in a large cloud of smoke – the third turbo failure for the weekend.

Moffat led by a large margin to Brock, another significant gap to McLeod (RX7), then Johnson. Moffat went on to win, 19 seconds ahead of Brock then another 20 seconds back to Johnson with McLeod about three seconds behind him in fourth.

Apparently Marsden announced to the media in attendance that the team would not be entering further races until we could find some reliability – his way of telling us he wasn't happy. We would miss the Surfers Paradise round and return for Oran Park nearly two months later.

It was really disappointing to feel we were being left behind at this stage in 1984 and very frustrating to be continually dealing with exploded turbochargers. We were running in the ragged edged margin between being competitive and being retired in a cloud of smoke, without having any way of knowing where on that edge we were. Sometimes 1.6 Bar of boost would win us a race, other times it would put us on the DNF list.

Points for the ATCC Driver's Championship after Wanneroo: Brock 73, Johnson 66, Moffat 45, McLeod 34, Richards 27, Grice 20, and Fury 15.

ATCC Round 4 Surfers Paradise Raceway, Queensland – May 12-13

As indicated we didn't attend this meeting, Howard opting to figuratively hold our noses to the grindstone back at Healey Road – figuratively because we heard and saw so little of him.

Once again though, Moffat set the pace early, locking up pole position with a 1:14.2, eight tenths of a second faster than his own track record. Masterton was next fastest with a 1:14.5 and then Johnson completed the front row of the grid with a 1:14.7. On the second row was Richards with 1:14.8 and Harvey in the HDT #05 car with 1:15.0. (Brock was OS competing at Silverstone, England in a Bob Jane sponsored Porsche 956 as a shakedown for his upcoming Le Mans attack.)

On Sunday Johnson got a blinder and jumped to a good lead from Harvey and then McLeod. The rain that had been threatening began to fall not long into the race. It was Johnson, Harvey, McLeod, Moffat for the first half. Then, still raining at about two thirds distance, with Johnson, McLeod and Moffat nose to tail, Moffat tried to out-brake McLeod at the end of the back straight but in the process was clipped by Wilmington's Falcon and spun way off the track in the slippery conditions. Harvey also got tangled up and stove into the bank that Moffat had narrowly managed to miss.

Moffat was finally stopped quite a long way from the track by a hidden tree stump that inflicted massive damage to the RX-7 and somewhat less serious damage to the driver. A broken finger, cracked sternum and heavy bruising would keep him from racing until Rnd 2 of the AEC in August.

Johnson finally won the race, to the delight of his many Queensland fans, approx. 3.5 seconds ahead of McLeod who was 25 seconds ahead of Gardner in the BMW.

Points score for the ATCC Driver's Championship after Surfers: Johnson 91, Brock 73, Richards 47, McLeod 57, Moffat 45, Grice 20, and Fury 15

ATCC Round 5 The Castrol Flying 50, Oran Park Raceway, NSW, May 26-27

Having returned from his race at Silverstone, Brock once again set the pace, putting #05 on pole with 1:14.3, Bob Morris in a State Building Society sponsored green and white RX-7 surprised with a next best of 1:14.5, then Masterton got his Falcon around in 1:14.8, good enough for third. Next were McLeod 1:15.0, Fury 1:15.1, Grice 1:15.3 and Johnson 1:15.4 making up the top nine who were all under the existing lap record. Moffat was still in bandages and did not appear. The weather was fine and quite hot all weekend.

In the race, Masterton jumped the start and was later penalized but he led down the big straight to the fast turn 1, closely attended by Brock, Johnson and Morris. Fury was leading a second gaggle with McLeod and Grice both pressing hard. Accounts of the incident varied but most agreed Fury and Grice were in a braking duel for turn 3 when Grice lost control and barrelled into Fury's front wheel, breaking the Bluebird's steering arm and putting an end to George's race. Richards was forced to stop at end lap 1 with brake line damage resulting from debris from this incident. Grice pitted at the end of the second lap but rejoined after his mudguard was dragged away from his LHF wheel.

Harrington retired his Commodore at the end of lap 3 with lost oil pressure and then Brock broke a tail shaft at the end of lap 8 and retired, putting paid to his slim title chances. The field was looking rather thin.

Bob Morris had impressed again, looking smooth and quick and staying away from the carnage. He won the 35-lap race by 11 seconds to McLeod who finished just one second ahead of Johnson. It had been a close and exciting race for those who survived the early drama.

Although a disastrous result here, following our efforts at Healey Road the Bluebird seemed competitive again, although far from dominant, and we were regaining some confidence.

Points score for the ATCC Driver's Championship after Oran Park, Johnson 111, McLeod 80, Brock 73, Richards 49, Moffat 45, Grice 31 and Fury 15.

ATCC Round 6 Lakeside Raceway, Brisbane, Queensland, June 16-17

It was a shame Howard was not in attendance at Lakeside as George finally broke the drought and pulled off our first ATCC round win. HM was in Japan again, allegedly to further discuss Nissan's plans for a Group A car for 1985.

"Queensland: Beautiful one day, perfect the next." Well, NO. Continuing the trend begun the previous year, Lakeside was again very wet! In fact at the end of Saturday's practice, water was flowing across the road at Australia's fastest corner and drains had to be dug in order to allow a race to take place on Sunday.

Jim Richards, New Zealander and master wet track driver impressed, putting the black BMW on pole with a 1:01.5, Johnson was next best with a 1:01.7, Fury third with 1:02.4, Harvey fourth with 1:04.0, and McLeod fifth. George claimed that his following lap, towards the end of the second session, would have been faster but apparently the organisers had packed away the timing equipment saying, *"you'd have to be nuts to try for a time in this lot!"*

The race began on a wet track with Richards bolting away from Johnson, Fury and Harvey at the end of lap 1. Fury got past Johnson on lap 6 and was harassing Richards for a lap before he passed and proceeded to take a strong lead. Johnson then took up the harassment of Richards. At half distance Johnson was catching Fury but George responded and then more rain fell – the gap extended again. Commodore driver Warren Cullen passed Richards for third position. The race wound down with Fury winning by around 20 seconds to Johnson, Cullen and Richards.

Early laps with George closing in on Johnson and Richards.

It had been a great drive by George in the wet conditions. Johnson was a strong second and secured the 1985 ATCC Driver's Championship with still one round to go.

Points score for the ATCC Driver's Championship after Lakeside: Johnson 134, McLeod 95, Richards 66, Brock 73, Moffat 45, Fury 40, and Grice 31.

ATCC Round 7 Motorcraft 100, Adelaide Raceway, South Australia, July 1

With brimming confidence following our last start win, Fury won pole with a scorching 56.1 second lap (two seconds under the lap record!), Grice, this time in a leased Roadways Commodore, claimed second, 1.2 seconds behind George, McLeod was third fastest on 57.5, then Brock then Johnson then Richards then Scott in the #16 Bluebird was seventh fastest with a 58.0. Moffat was again absent due to his injuries.

Having turned down the boost ever so slightly for the race, from the Glen Dix start flag, Johnson got a blinder from the third row and led Fury into turn 1 – Scott back in tenth. Grice managed to get passed Fury for a brief interval before George re-took second and was soon all over the back of Johnson. He passed him at end of the main straight and moved away to a three second lead. Brock then harassed and found a way past Johnson.

On lap 11, with Fury easing back a little, the Bluebird's turbocharger must have thought its work was done for the day and it expired with the usual telltale plume of blue-ish smoke, leaving Brock in the lead from Grice then Johnson then Scott. Welcome back Howard.

Grice managed to get past Brock at about half distance and he went on to win with Brock close behind and Johnson only half a second further back after 35 laps of very tight racing. Gary Scott placed a fine and steady fourth about two seconds further back.

Final points score for the ATCC series: Johnson 134 (corrected to drop lowest score), Brock 96, McLeod 95, Cullen 91 (corrected), Richards 77, Grice 56, Moffat 45 and Fury 40.

We'd pushed the turbocharger to its limit and often past it in this series and George was let down twice (Wanneroo while running a clear second and Adelaide while leading strongly late in the race) and at Oran Park he was taken out by Grice again. Had he stayed in that race and not advanced further he'd have placed third. So allowing for the 'ifs and buts' it's conceivable he'd have finished the series with at least 108 points, a very strong second to Dick Johnson who'd had quite an extraordinary season, finishing every round on the podium.

What actually happened though was a very competitive championship series with six different winners. Of the top runners only BMW failed to win a race and only Brock won two. As the final Group C Touring Car Championship in Australia it had been a fitting tribute.

1984 AUSTRALIAN ENDURANCE CHAMPIONSHIP

AEC Round 1 The Silastic 300, Amaroo Park, Sydney, NSW, August 4-5

For this his thirteenth start at Amaroo Park that year, Gary Scott in BB1 as car #16, won pole position with a 52.2 second lap, followed by Richards and then McLeod. Christine Gibson took a place near the back of the field. It had been decided to leave the #15 Bluebird in Melbourne and use the Sydney-based cars, Bluebird #16 and the EXA #60 for the Amaroo race that kicked off the '84 AEC. Scott was given the drive as a reward for success in the AMSCAR Series that year as well as to help prepare for his partnering George at Bathurst.

Gary Scott remembers:

*"Do you remember the morning of the CRC 300... the car wouldn't start for the warm-up? It turned out to be a really simple electrical issue and Howard let me talk him into allowing me to take it for a test run up the Annangrove public road, I remember pulling flat out in 4th gear and then had to drive back into the circuit with all the punters and people staring at me and the car. When I got to the ticket box entry, Ivan Stibbard's[3] P.A. just said " You are f**ing joking!!"*

I didn't remember, but it was too good a story to leave out!

---
3 Chief of the ARDC.

The race was run in wet conditions once again and Scott, the only one of the top contenders to take the gamble to begin on slicks, led from the start but was over-taken by Richards' BMW during the first lap. Brock came from fifth to overtake Scott relegating him to third on about lap 12. Ron Gillard in one of the RX-7s then also worked his way past Scott pushing Gary back another place. Christine's EXA was lapped on lap 17.

Finnigan's now Repco Accessories sponsored Commodore worked his way past Brock and then took the lead from Richards. Brock then passed Richards into second place with Finnigan drawing away in the lead. On lap 25 Scott had overtaken the Mazda to be fourth and, as the track dried, was better placed on his dry tyres and proceeded to go past Richards on lap 31 and then Brock on lap 42. Most pitstops took place around lap 45.

Richards retired about lap 47 with a broken stub axle. Then rain again began to fall on about lap 50. Brock headed for the pits on lap 62 but hit a puddle in the entrance and ploughed into the armco.

More drama as Finnigan spun at Lake Corner and let Scott through to the lead on about lap 63. The EXA hit the wall coming onto pit straight on lap 67 and Christine retired a lap later. Finnigan hit the wall and retired on lap 69.

Scott changed to intermediates[4] at his scheduled stop on lap 70 and returned to the race in second place behind Harrop in Commodore #8 who pitted for full service straight after. This put Scott back in the lead.

The race was shortened from 155 to 140 laps due to the weather, much slower lap times and consequent concern about the race not finishing before darkness descended. Gary Scott led from lap 63 to win by 20 seconds, Harrop placed second and McLeod third.

It was a copybook race by Scott and Marsden with just the single, scheduled pitstop and a well judged pace to allow a one-minute lead to slowly deteriorate and Scott to win by 20 seconds. It was also a very exciting and interesting race as you might have gathered, further enhanced for me by

My two motorsport bosses speaking to the world while I converse with Gary.

---
4   Lightly grooved tyres suitable for light rain conditions.

being on radio duty conveying messages to and from the car.

Gary's recollections of the race included:

"Starting the Silastic 300 at Amaroo on slicks on a soaking wet track and keeping it on the island – I actually led for nearly a lap and remember power sliding in top gear going through the uphill kink on the way to Bitupave Hill lap after lap!"

After Round 1 of the AEC Driver's Championship, Gary Scott led on 25 points with McLeod second on 20. For the Manufacturers title, Nissan led on 25, Mazda and BMW second with 20 points each and Holden with 11 and Ford 9.

AEC Round 2 The Valvoline 250, Oran Park, Sydney, NSW, August 18-19

Allan Moffat made his comeback to racing for this round and while he was under the weather with a dose of the flu, it seemed he hadn't lost any speed and proceeded to quickly lodge a 1:13.1 to claim pole position. Inspired by Gary Scott's win in Round 1, George did almost as well in putting the #15 Bluebird on the front row alongside Moffat with a 1:13.3.

Sitting behind these two little-engined cars were two of the biggest-engined ones, the XE Falcons of Dick Johnson, 1:13.6 and Steve Masterton, 1:13.7. Jim Richards' BMW had the inside running on the third row with a 1:13.9. Grice had his rented Roadways Commodore on row 4 alongside McLeod, Brock and Perkins were in Europe again racing their Porsche but Harvey had the #05 car on the fifth row.

It was a classy field set up ready to race on the newly renovated Oran Park Grand Prix circuit, it was a beautiful day and the crowds had turned out in abundance.

At flag-fall Johnson made a fantastic start and managed to squeeze past both Moffat and Fury by the turn 1 kink and managed to survive the braking dual into turn 2. Masterton also blasted past Fury to be third by lap's end.

Looking good off the start line but Johnson's Falcon is about to blast though that gap and into the lead.

By lap 5 Moffat had recovered from the surprise of being swallowed whole by Johnson's Falcon and was reeling him back in. He managed to sneak past on lap 15. Johnson seemed to be slowing and allowed Masterton to also get by him and then also Fury. Strangely the green Falcon seemed to recover from whatever ailed it and the race settled somewhat to Moffat (increasing his lead slowly), Masterton, Fury, Johnson.

First to falter of the leaders was Fury at around lap 30 – the Bluebird had a head gasket fail – our first sign we had troubles in this area, and he was out. Masterton then had a similar problem and he too was sidelined.

The racers began to realize they were in an endurance race and calmed down a notch with Moffat well clear of Johnson then Harvey but then the #05 car broke its gearbox and retired on lap 43. Moffat stopped for fuel on lap 51 and surprised all by swapping Hansford into the driver's seat, all in 40 seconds. Moffat must have been flagging due to his bout of the flu. Hansford came out of the pits 20 seconds behind Johnson who was due to make his own stop. Grice was well back in third and slowing.

Johnson made a 45 second stop for fuel and tyres on lap 55 giving Hansford a break that was not to be challenged and also let Richards squeak through into second. On fresh rubber though, Johnson quickly took that place back. That was how the race wound down with Hansford being able to respond to each of Johnson's efforts to close the gap.

At the end of this weekend the progressive score for the AEC Driver's Championship was McLeod on 31, Scott 25, Johnson 23, Richards 20, Moffat and Hansford 12.5 each.

For the Manufacturers Title, Mazda 45, Ford 32, Holden 21, Nissan 25, BMW 20.

AEC Round 3 The Castrol 500, Sandown Raceway, Victoria, September 8-9

The Light Car Club of Australia finally but proudly unveiled their just redeveloped motor racing facility at Sandown Park, south east of Melbourne, for the first endurance 500km race – 129 laps of the newly extended 3.878km 'international circuit'. The increase from 3.1kms to 3.878kms was achieved with

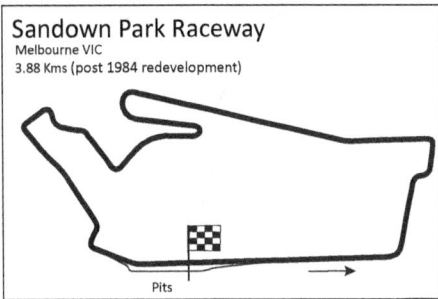

Sandown Park Raceway
Melbourne VIC
3.88 Kms (post 1984 redevelopment)

Pits

a new quite tight section in the infield at the northern (Dandenong Road) end. The redevelopment also featured a much-needed new pit area, (moved from between turns one and two at the southern end of the circuit to just north of the grandstand on the main straight.)

Whereas Sandown had always been a circuit favouring the V8s these changes provided some balance, in theory giving the lighter, better handling and stopping cars a chance to shine. Where the long, uphill back straight had fed into a very fast sweeping left-hander, it now led to a hard stop for a left hand almost hairpin which was followed very soon after by a definitely first gear hairpin right-hander. Working out a suitable set of gear ratios caused consternation for all teams.

The debut of the EXA Turbo. In the pits during early practice.

This meeting was also the debut of the new VK Commodore, in the Holden Dealer Team's case, in a very striking new dayglo red and white paint scheme. This car would have rather a short but glorious life as the Group C class was to be done away with at the end of the year.

Most teams agreed the track would get faster after some rubber was laid down on the new section, so leaving their best efforts in qualifying to the second session but Fury apparently didn't get the memo and quickly did a 1:46.2, a time that would see #15 on pole and which remains to this day, the fastest ever touring car lap on the 3.878 km international circuit.

The job of the intercooler on a forced induction car is to cool, and thereby make more dense, the charge air coming from the turbocharger's compressor. As long as the correct air to fuel ratio is maintained, more dense air equals more power. So accordingly a plot was hatched. The on-board fire extinguisher system, part of which was directed under the bonnet, was diverted to the front of the intercooler and a 5kg fire extinguisher could be triggered to dump through the intercooler via a beautifully Pete-made spray bar attached to it's front. Using this setup we could further cool the compressed air from the turbo to near zero degrees. It was all nicely plumbed and fitted so we could easily remove the system before the race but in qualifying the system could be triggered going up the back straight hill for example I don't think there was any regulation disallowing this and it seemed to deliver the goods.

In session two Grice did a 1:46.3 in the Roadways Commodore to win second place alongside George on the grid, then Johnson claimed the inside of row two with a 1:46.9 with Brock alongside him, one tenth slower. Moffat and Gardner filled row three. Due to the 500km race distance a minimum of two drivers were required and most teams used their upcoming Bathurst pairing. Accordingly George Fury was teamed with Gary Scott.

When the flag fell on Sunday, morning Fury got away well but both

he and Grice were swamped by Johnson and Brock as they arrived at turn 1, sending most in the packed grandstand into raptures, if not the much smaller group of Japcar fans (supporters of the 'rice-burners' as they were called before political correctness became a thing). As usual, with the adrenaline pumping, the first few corners were rather untidy as cars touched and bounced around but they sorted themselves out up the back straight. Moffat, who'd got mixed up in the rough stuff, was back in tenth place.

Grice was on the charge and got past Fury on lap 3. As the race settled, Johnson led from Brock and then Grice, with a widening gap back to Harvey, Fury and Moffat – it seemed at this stage that Sandown was still a V8 circuit. Johnson was out front and appeared to be going away from Brock who was falling back into clutches of Grice who squeezed past him on lap 13. Moffat had by then recovered and gotten passed Fury and Harvey – Fury having been able to get the better of the HDT #25 car. George managed to get back on Moffat's tail and they raced hard together for quite some time, allowing Harvey to close and join the fray. This was not endurance style racing!

On lap 32 though, Fury was out. The engine block had cracked in the top surface, through one of the stud holes, causing head gasket leakage and overheating. (You can read more about this in the section on engine development from page 169.

Pitstops began on lap 34 with Brock's crew doing a slick refuel and tyre change and getting Perkins belted in and back on the track in eighth place. With fresh tyres he was quickly back among the leaders. Then Johnson pitted on lap 37 but his stop was to retire as he'd shredded his gearbox – all that horsepower through first and second gears each lap had proved too much. The only other car to have led the race, the brand new Roadways Racing VK Commodore of Grice/Steve Harrington, also stopped with a broken gearbox while running second on lap 103 of 129. Grice had the consolation of setting the fastest lap before he expired.

Together with regular co-driver and HDT team manager Larry Perkins, Brock won his ninth and last Sandown long distance race. The pair finished a lap ahead of the Moffat/Hansford RX-7 with the second HDT Commodore of John Harvey and new team recruit David Parsons finishing third, a further lap adrift.

As this was the only Group C touring car race ever held on the new longer international circuit, Grice's lap of 1:48.3 remains the Group C lap record for the circuit and Fury's pole time of 1:46.2 the fastest ever lap.

Following Round 3 the progressive score for the AEC Driver's title was Moffat and Hansford on 35.5 each, McLeod on 31, Brock, Perkins and Scott all on 25.

For the Manufacturers' Title, Mazda 68, Holden 46, Ford 43, Nissan still on 25, BMW still on 20.

See the section on Engine and turbocharger development beginning page 169 regarding the final stage of the turbocharger evolution before Bathurst.

AEC Round 4 The James Hardie 1000 at Bathurst, NSW, September 29-30

Team accommodation was again at The Knickerbocker Hotel in Bathurst but I think we were too pumped to play up much in 1984.

Except that, when we arrived on the Saturday before the race weekend, Smithy and Den got the idea that a game of golf could be in order. I'll let George tell you:

"Nissan Australia had just released a range of promotional merchandise which included golf balls carrying the Nissan moniker. They had a part number something like 99999-34567.

Den and I conjured up a plan and on the Monday morning, we rang Ronnie Motorsport, who was then still back at Healey Road, and placed an urgent order for 36 part no. 99999-34567 for immediate dispatch by airfreight to the Nissan Motorsport facility C/- Bathurst paddock.

We had a good relationship with John Pickstock, the manager of the Parts warehouse and knew he'd play along so we told Ronnie to contact him. Being very efficient when on a mission, Ron raced over to parts and hounded John, "I urgently need 36, 99999-34567 handpicked now as the race team is in urgent need of these parts up at Bathurst.

The parts boys stuffed him around and got his dander up but sure enough, a day or so later they arrived." Poor Ronnie.

In the lead-up to qualifying a Toledo Tools Professional Pit Stop Competition was conducted and telecast. Our team was the comprehensive winner taking a tad over 18 seconds to change four wheels and dump a churn of fuel. A happy looking crew was presented with a large (by the

A happy and proud team receiving the Toledo 'trophy'.

standards of the day) Toledo toolbox, which we put to good use for the rest of the season.

Just three weeks before Bathurst we received notification from CAMS'

At Healey Rd workshops near ready to head off to Bathurst. #15 in foreground is BB#3, looking rather sad at not getting a run is BB#2, and down the end, set up as the 'T' car, is the original BB#1.

George receives his pole trophy from the James Hardie GM.

Car #15 gets to share the limelight too.

On Saturday night Howard and George are presented with a Bed Post Trophy at a Nissan Dealer celebration in the hospitality marquee, set up in the paddock.

THE STORY – 1984

Front row of the grid – the flag is up…

Charging up to Hell Corner with George in the lead but Masterton spots an opening and goes for it…

…putting the big squeeze on Moffat.

George out-brakes Brock down into Murray's.

George arrives for the first scheduled stop.

Fury out, Scott in, while a flurry of activity prepares #15 for the next hour.

In the paddock for a diff change after it failed on lap 80. George sits strapped in contemplating what might have been.

Gary doing a stint.

that we could run the modified T04 turbocharger we'd developed. As we hoped it might, the restricted compressor inlet and exhaust outlet made it easy for CAMS to approve, even though Howard made rather a fuss of how he'd finally cajoled CAMS into this concession.

Thursday and Friday on the mountain proceeded without major incident, George qualified the #15 car second fastest to Brock, Christine Gibson in the EXA now running as #16, managed 26th fastest (better at least than the Bluebirds' 1981 31st and 43rd grid positions, and we were all in good spirits and looking forward to Hardies Heroes on Saturday morning, especially with our extra charge cooling 'accessory' up our sleeve – just the thing for a fast trip up the mountain. As it turned out though we woke on Saturday morning to the coldest Bathurst day on record and our magic trick was not required.

As per the now well-established procedure, with live National TV coverage each of the fastest 10 qualifiers, beginning with 10th, would do a warm up lap then a timed fast lap. When it was George's turn, Dick Johnson had just done a 2:14.710 – three tenths faster than his qualifying time and the quickest thus far. George then laid down a stunning 2:13.850, almost one full second faster than his qualifying time and thereby setting a Group C Touring Car lap record that would never be beaten! Brock was last to run but could only manage 2:14.039, also three tenths quicker than his qualifying time but only good enough for second place on the grid. Four-cylinder turbocharged engines had finally arrived!

The grid for Sunday had been set with George on pole, the first time in the seven-year history of Hardies Heroes that pole had been won by a non-V8 engined car.

Next to George on the front row would be the crowd firm favourite, Peter Brock in his still new luminescent red VK Commodore #05. On row two would sit Dick Johnson's ever-so-bright-green, Palmer Tube Mills XE Falcon #17 alongside Allan Grice's white and yellow SAAS sponsored Roadways VK Commodore. On row three would be #43, Allan Moffat in the first of the diminutive Peter Stuyvesant Mazda RX-7s together with Jim Richards' immaculate black, JPS BMW 635i. Steve Masterton in the Masterton Homes Falcon and Gregg Hansford in the second Stuyvesant Mazda #42 would make up row four and on row 5 would be #41, Bob Morris in a very smart looking RW1 sponsored Mazda RX-7 with Tom Walkinshaw's big 12-cylinder Jaguar XJ-S, #12 completing the top 10 and encompassing a record six marques, Nissan, Holden, Ford, Mazda, BMW and Jaguar. What a sight!

Sunday dawned clear and bright and promised great things. After all the festivities, pom-pom twirling, the command to 'START YOUR ENGINES', etc. etc., George made a brilliant start and led Brock down to Hell Corner and up the mountain. Tragically though for all concerned, not least of all our team, there was mayhem back on the starting grid as the last of our top 10 destroyed its clutch on take-off and did not move. The Walkinshaw Jag was hit hard from behind by car #62, a Camaro that had started from the back row of the grid and was, by the time it got to row 5, almost up to racing speed. The Jag was spun into the path of Peter Williamson's Group A Toyota Supra which had also accelerated all the way from the back of the grid. The track was completely blocked with wrecked cars.

In the meantime, Masterton who'd been on the fourth row bolted up alongside Moffat from row 3 and then pushed him across, almost upending the much smaller Mazda over the pit wall. Needless to say the race was red-flagged and those who'd gotten away before the chaos began trundling back to the pits to await the big clean up and to get set for a second start.

Unfortunately Fury was not able to duplicate his flawless first start and needed a second and then a third dump of the clutch to get going and he was fourth into turn 1 behind Brock, Johnson and Grice and with Harvey close behind. Over the next few laps Harvey passed Fury and then, another couple of laps later, he also got past Grice until…

A lap or so later, Fury snuck up the inside of Grice coming out of Hell Corner and surprised Harvey when George was suddenly beside him as he attempted to resume the left side of the track. Harvey's reaction sent him off the outside of the track and he lost two positions. The inside running proved a slower line for George however and that allowed Grice back in front.

Moffat retired #43 Mazda on lap 15 due to an unspecified engine failure, possibly related to the collision with the pit wall in the first start. In a move I hadn't seen before, he and Hansford entered and qualified two cars but with only one driver each. We'll never know how they'd have handled driver duties[5] for the rest of the race had one of them not expired but Moffat simply stepped in as second driver in #42 car.

At 19 laps it was Brock leading Johnson then Grice and then Fury, Harvey and Moffat/Hansford in the remaining Stuyvesant RX-7.

Grice led briefly on lap 35 when Brock made his first stop. Then on lap 40, Richards' BMW dropped a valve thereby trashing his engine.

Four laps later Harrington, driving the Grice car, had a big lose exiting Hell Corner and stove into the tyre barrier. He walked back to the pits to be met by an angry Grice who proceeded to run to the car, get it started and drive it back to the pits. Unfortunately it proved non-repairable and they took no further part.

Just before Johnson's scheduled stop he managed to catch and pass Perkins in #05 to take the lead on lap 45. French who then took over from Johnson was not able to match Perkin's pace and #05 went on its merry way.

At 69 laps it was Brock/Perkins, Johnson/French, Fury/Scott, Cullen/Jones, Moffat/Hansford. On lap 80, just shy of half distance however, Fury's crown wheel and pinion cried enough and car #15 was taken back to our garage for a diff replacement. Four dumps of the clutch from the start line had been at least one too many. George Smith took charge of the diff change and Fury was very soon back in the race, albeit some laps down and out of contention.

Johnson's Falcon stopped on the way up the mountain on lap 100 and had to be trucked back to the pits. His crew got it going again by replacing the fuel pressure regulator in short order and Dick resumed, only to break an axle on lap 129, this time resulting in his retirement.

With eight laps to go, it was Brock/Perkins, Cullen/Jones and Harvey/Parsons, all Commodores followed by the Moffat/Hansford RX-7. On the penultimate lap Cullen/Jones had to pit costing them two positions and on the final lap Brock slowed to a near crawl to allow Harvey to close the gap, engineering the perfect 1-2 for the HDT, albeit with two laps separating them.

So, after a rather boring second half (for us at least), it was Brock/Perkins, 163 laps, followed by Harvey/Parsons, Moffat/Hansford and Cullen/Jones all with 161 laps. Fury was seen late in the telecast passing the Brock/Perkins car to claim back a lap and at race end was placed 16th with 146 laps completed.

---

5   Regulations dictated that each car had to have at least two drivers.

Christine Gibson with Glenn Seton in the EXA Turbo, who'd managed to get past the stationary Jaguar before the carnage began, managed 76 laps before a failed layshaft bearing in the gearbox put them on the DNF list.

My job at pitstops was to change the LH front wheel. One of Howard's jobs was to stop the car at the correct mark on the pavement – Bluebird half a car forward of the EXA.

Somewhere around one third distance Fury came in for a scheduled stop and I removed his left front, dumped it against the pit-wall, bolted on the new wheel and he was off. The EXA arrived as George left and was stopped at Fury's mark so that what I grabbed to put on when I spun around was Fury's just removed wheel. The EXA left the pits with one much larger front wheel than the other and had to be brought back in on the following lap to have that corrected. I think Seton was steering at the time and, when told to come back in, he said something like, I thought it felt weird. How embarrassing.

Glen in for an unscheduled second LHF tyre change.

I don't remember Howard apologising for stopping the EXA in the wrong spot but then apologizing was not something he did. Oh well, it made no difference and George's compliment that I'd given him a great engine, more than made up for it.

Not that there was much interest from our camp by this stage but, for the record, points for the AEC Drivers' title after Bathurst were, Moffat and Hansford on 55.5 each, Brock and Perkins 50 each, Harvey 43, McLeod 31 and Scott 27.

For the Manufacturers Title, Holden 96, Mazda 88, Ford 51, Nissan 27, BMW still 20.

Approaching The Cutting with Bathurst as a scenic backdrop.

AEC Round 5 The Motorcraft 300 Surfers Paradise Raceway Qld, Nov 3-4

There was a palpable tension in the air leading up to this final race of the 1984 AEC as both Drivers and Manufacturers titles were still up for grabs – well, between Mazda and GMH anyway.

Grice surprised and impressed early with a pole grabbing 1:14.0. Moffat's first time back at Surfers after his big crash here in 1983, was also impressive, claiming second place on the grid with 1:14.2, then Masterton got third place on the front row with 1:14.3. Gary Scott driving BB3, rather confusingly running as #16, took fourth with 1:14.4, Greg Hansford in the second Stuyvesant RX-7 matched Gary's time to be fifth, then Brock with 1:14.6 and Johnson with 1:14.7, unusually back in sixth and seventh. Fury joined the pit crew!

Moffat, Masterton, Scott, Brock, Grice, Johnson. So far so good.

On Sunday, Masterton made a great start and slid by Moffat into the lead as they went through the sweeper under the bridge for the first time. Moffat was followed by Scott in #16, which was in turn followed by Grice who'd not started so well. Scott was soon passed by Brock who joined a spirited tussle between Masterton and Moffat for several laps. Moffat was a clear leader by lap 20.

Dick Johnson, though on his home circuit, did not seem to be able to match the pace of the Masterton Falcon or the lighter Commodores at this meeting but then broke his gearbox, had it replaced, and then broke its replacement! Not his weekend.

Masterton was forced to retire when his Watts link broke away from the diff housing on lap 19.

Scott made his scheduled stop for fuel and tyres (with George Fury on right hand rear rattle gun), the quick stop drew applause from HM. Brock caught and passed Moffat to take the lead shortly before their pitstops.

Late in the race Scott, having rapidly caught Moffat, was attempting a pass for second place but there was a coming together and Scott was forced to retire with a bent steering arm late in the race. 4. Gary's account of this incident is slightly at odds with some commentators: *"Remember Moffat deliberately driving into me at Surfers Paradise in the final Group C Race of 1984?"*

With a huge storm threatening, Brock continued to draw away and at race end was more than a minute ahead of Moffat followed by Hansford. Brock had won the battle but Mazda the war. The presentation was held in tropical downpour, Moffat not bothering to get out of his car.

For the AEC Manufacturer's Title, Mazda had narrowly won with a total of 111 points to Holden's 108, Ford's 60, Nissan's 27 and BMW's 20.

The Driver's Title went to Moffat on 78.5, with Hansford second on 75.5, then Brock on 75, Harvey on 56 and Perkins with 50. Despite expectations Brock couldn't really expect to win a title if he took a couple of meetings off to go racing overseas.

As crews were packing up to leave the circuit following this last Group C Touring Car title race, the storm clouds parted and bright sunshine poured forth, maybe heralding an end to the rancour that had characterised this class of racing in recent times.

From my point of view, after some years struggling with little success to triumph against Mitsubishi with their Lancers in rallying, it was galling to have spent the last three years struggling to be competitive with, but getting our bums caned by another Japanese behemoth – Mazda.

As a last hurrah, following the success and popularity of the 40-lap Touring Car race with compulsory pitstop at the '83 Australian Grand Prix, it was decided to repeat this event at our home circuit in '84 This would turn out to be the last AGP held at Calder Raceway before it became a round of the Formula One series and was moved to the Adelaide street circuit.

Australian Grand Prix, Touring Car Trophy support race, Calder Park Raceway, November 17-18

This Australian Grand Prix support race was to be the penultimate race meeting for the Bluebirds running under 'NISSAN', and rather eerily, had a near identical result to the previous year.

Déjà vu must have been the theme for this meeting as the AGP was again won by Roberto Moreno in a Ralt RT4. Second this time though was Keke Rosberg and third Andrea de Cesaris, both also in Ralt RT4s.

Following the main event was again a 40-lap race for tourers with a compulsory pitstop where two tyres were required to be changed. Once again each car was required to stop on a nominated lap.

George again lined up in pole position and, just as in '83 and at Bathurst that year, Brock was alongside in his dayglo red and white VK Commodore.

This time, when the flag fell, George bolted away from the line and was first into turn 1, leaving Brock in his wake. I've not been able to find any information about our pitstop but it can't have been too shabby as Fury was never headed and won convincingly. Brock second, Warren Cullen in the K-mart Commodore third and, as a pointer to the future, Jim Richards won the Group A Class in the black BMW.

Fury led a hard-fought race from Go to Whoa.

It was Brock's only loss in four races in his #05 dayglo Group C, VK Commodore.

Touring Car Cup, Baskerville Raceway, Tasmania, November 25

Still thinking the team would be running Group A Skylines in 1985 and planning to build a team around George Fury and young Glen Seton, HM thought he'd better give Seton some turbocharged race miles in the Bluebird before the '84 season wrapped up. (There's that Sydney connection at work again.)

Barry Bray was keen to do the Sports Sedan races at Baskerville too so the pantech was loaded up with the #15 Bluebird and Bazza's 2-door Stanza and put on the Bass Straight ferry[6]. Howard, George Smith, Dennis and Bazza flew over on an Ansett flight. Glen's father Barry (Bo) was promised a flight too and HM told him there'd be a ticket waiting for him at Sydney airport. There wasn't of course so Bo bought his own.

Bazza's Stanza at Healey Road ready to go to Tassy.

Glen hadn't previously driven a car with a dog engagement gearbox and there was much crunching going on for some laps in practice. I'm told he had to come to a full stop a couple of times (unable to successfully shift down) and start anew in first. Apparently he got the hang of it eventually and was able to post a time for the start grid.

It's recorded that there were only six Group C cars in attendance but that didn't prevent Seton and Harrington coming together in the race and #15 recording another DNF. It was won by Allan Grice in a Roadways Racing Commodore.

---

6   The Princess of Tasmania

For the record, we had 111 race starts including 16 for the EXA. 29 of the 111 total were heat starts in the AMSCAR series. We had 33 DNFs including six from blown turbochargers while racing and nine from crashes (race incidents). We had 10 outright wins, eight seconds and six thirds – 24 times on the podium.

Fury won five races and started from pole six times. Gibson won two AMSCAR heats and was on pole for one AMSCAR round (but failed to start in all three heats that day). Scott won three races including two AMSCAR heats and started from pole four times including one AMSCAR round (three starts).

If only we'd had one more season with the Bluebirds running under Group C, I'm sure we could have cleaned up. Oh well.

1985...

The first DR30 Skyline race car we'd built as time allowed during 1984 was near completion when we received a rude shock. As well as a huge amount of other work, as part of the development, George Smith and Barry Bray had designed, made a mock-up, and had cast and machined at huge expense, aluminium front suspension uprights. Howard was to arrange for these and other components to be homologated for the DR30 Skyline.

The #1 DR30 Skyline near completion at Healey Road.

Also around this time, late 1984, Barry had organised a holiday to Japan. When he arrived and visited Nissan's competition department at Oppama, he was rather shocked to learn that Nissan Japan had already homologated front uprights for the DR30 and in fact many other parts during their own development of the Skyline for motorsport. He immediately called Howard back in Australia to report. *"Better we keep that between ourselves Barry"* was HM's response.

Later, after the homologation story had come out in Australia, as it inevitably had to (we'd have loved to have been a fly on the wall when he explained all that to the higher powers), Howard arrived at our workshop one day, I believe around Easter '85, to explain that Nissan was suffering a downturn and was on a cost-cutting campaign – they could no longer afford the racing budget. Fred would be taking over the team, so we were given the choice of transferring to his employ or accepting a dismissal payment based on our time with the company, and leave.

My memory was that we all opted to leave but I now understand that George Smith and Dennis Watson, both with young families, chose to stay on initially. Two or three months later after they'd arranged alternative jobs, they also abandoned ship.

I'd had 13 years with Nissan so my payout was significant, making my decision a no-brainer.

Nissan had pulled the pin on the Australian race team, gifting it to Fred Gibson who would take over the lease on our premises and ownership of what it contained – but with no eligible car to race. Howard accepted a job in the UK with Nissan's sports car racing program some time not long afterward. When asked by Muscle Car magazine about the arrangement to take over the team, Fred said, *"I thought I was just going to come down and manage it, but when I came down to see Howard, he said: Oh no, if you're happy to take it over, I've found $750,000 from Peter Jackson for you, so you take it over and run it." It blew me away. Whatever was there (in the workshop) was mine!"* The follow up question from MC mag was: *"Was it a $1 contract or something?"*, Fred responded, *"Contract? Howard would never have a contract. There was no paperwork with Howard. Just all of a sudden I was asking Christine if she wanted to go and live in Melbourne because Howard has just given us the race team."*

As if to emphasise this point, Bazza Bray told us once that he'd been in Howard's office one time at the end of the work day and he swept all the paperwork on his desk into the waste paper basket then picked up his briefcase to leave. *"Don't you need any of that?"* asked Baz incredulously. *"If it's important someone will get back to me about it,"* was the response as he led them out the door. No wonder the race cars' log books were twice lost.

A significant number of equipment items in our workshop had been purchased by team members (mostly Jamie) who'd several times invested his own money when equipment he needed, had been denied by HM as too expensive. His shock absorber dyno being an example.

The engine dynamometer I'd used so much for our development on both rally and race engines over the years was located some ten kilometres away in Moorabbin and when it's owner wanted to retire and sell the business, back in 1977, Jamie, Les Collins and myself raised the funds to buy the business so we could continue to have use of the facility. After Fred took over the Healey Road workshop he bought and installed his own engine dyno for new engine man, Bo Seton. So much for his harping that we'd spent a way too vast amount of Nissan's money. Maybe it's OK when a cigarette company is chipping in buckets of cash.

The DR30 Skyline we built was apparently modified to comply with the homologation done by Nissan in Japan and it, together with two other second hand DR30 race cars Fred bought from the U.K., went on to run successfully in Group A racing in Australia from 1986 with these and the later Skylines, including the R32 'Godzilla', that followed.

Early 1987 I accepted a job at Dick Johnson Racing as engine man shortly after he began his Ford Sierra Turbo program. The Sierra had a two-litre twin-cam, Cosworth-developed motor but it also had an identical T3 Garrett turbocharger to the standard Bluebird and I was faced with nearly all the same problems and frustrations we'd battled during the Bluebird program, including regular smoky turbocharger blow-ups. This all felt like a huge retrograde step and I really struggled to get my heart into it – I should never have taken it on. I asked to be replaced just nine months later, shortly before the team headed to Bathurst.

It wasn't until the release of the RS500 Sierra with it's much larger Garrett T04 turbocharger and injectors, and the arrival of the hot-up kits shortly before I departed, that the car became competitive and in fact went on to dominate Group A racing in 1988. I was pleased to be out though.

1987 with DJR. Gregg Hansford coming into the pits at Surfers Paradise Raceway with a failed turbocharger in his pre-evolution Ford Sierra Turbo.

Bluebird development

In reading articles about the Nissan Sport Bluebirds I'm struck by the number of times Howard is given credit for winning freedoms from CAMS for various modifications, Fred Gibson in particular pushes this line, for example, *"Howard was amazing at getting these homologation things through."* This is such a travesty. There were very few examples of HM winning us freedoms, in fact I would not be shocked to discover there wasn't a single example.

In a 2018 edition of Muscle Car magazine, when asked "Did the boys in the workshop do dodgy stuff that you wouldn't know about?", Fred replied, *"They probably did. They ran the whole thing. I'm not knocking them. With no direction, to do what they did themselves, [well] they all did a good job. I suppose what they didn't do was read the rule book, though the rules were pretty flexible in those days..."*

This speaks volumes, though in fact we actually *pored* over that rule book, and usually found an angle to get the result we needed 'within the letter of the law'[1] or, at the least, in a way that wasn't going to get us in trouble.

The home of the Bluebirds' development program, George Smith presiding.

When speaking with the media Howard had a way of taking credit for innovation while sounding humble and leaving the impression he was just being magnanimous when he gave credit to 'the boys' – it wasn't that they were clever, more that I'm so good at getting the concessions we want from CAMS. He was absolutely masterful at this but also at charming and distracting officials when required!

Regarding the handling and drivability of the Bluebirds, Fred said, *"It wasn't a very good handling car. It was always a difficult car to drive, a nervous car to drive."* Gary Scott's impression was somewhat different – when asked, *"What was it like to drive generally?"* he said,

---

1   ...excepting the oversize engine incident that happened as a result of intense frustration that we couldn't get HM to go into bat for us regarding a turbo allowance ;-)

"Fabulous. It was just a brilliant car... It would go exactly where you pointed it. We had it very well sorted." George Fury seemed to think it was OK too. When asked the same question, he said, "It ended up being the best touring car I've driven. The Skylines weren't as good. They [the BBs] might have been hard to drive early on but at the end of its life the Bluebird was magic, a nice car to drive."

George Smith takes up the Bluebird development story:
"Getting two new cars to the grid for the 1981 Bathurst race was an accomplishment in itself but I remember issues requiring some serious additional work arising almost immediately. One of the recurring driver comments was, "too much understeer, I mean plough understeer. I have to back off the throttle or run off the road."

FRONT SUSPENSION

Fred had been asking for heavier and heavier front springs to deal with the understeer and Jamie had been running back and forth to the spring maker, finally getting to the point of having 1400lb springs in the front of the car which was just ridiculous. George Smith and Jamie came to the conclusion that the car had a roll centre problem. The following is his story about its resolution.

"The initial change that 'improved' the understeer problem was an increase in the front spring and anti roll bar rate – by heaps!

"We'd all had experience with McPherson Strut front suspension in rallying (myself with Ford Escort and then Datsun Stanzas). While the rally cars had a ride-height similar to your everyday road car, the first thing on the list for a circuit car build was to set ride height 'as low as possible' as practical' taking into consideration we had a regulation 4" CAMS Ride Height Block to drive over when scrutineered pre and post race. [See our own 'go-no go' gauge for ground clearance stored in the transporter, page 73]

We couldn't at first work out what was going on and in conversation with Jamie, I said I'd have a word with Carroll Smith, the engineer Allan Moffat contracted in 1977 to come out from the US to build and engineer the XC Falcons for that year. I'm proud to have been a part of that team in '77.

DEVELOPMENT – FRONT SUSPENSION

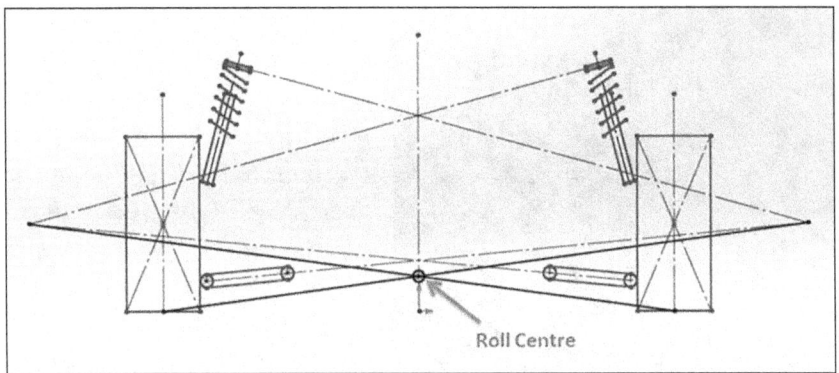

Mapping the front Roll Centre: If the body of the car is lowered, the bottom suspension arms will likely be angled down toward the centre of the car and this will have a dramatic affect on the location of the roll centre, and therefore the handling, especially as the body leans in cornering.

Carroll was back in Australia engineering the Masterton Homes Falcon at this time – I put the problem to him.

His reply was: "Well those McPherson Struts can be a real cow of a thing and I see you run the car pretty low. Go back to the shop and make a scale model of your chassis including the front suspension, measure the static roll centre height, then roll the model chassis one degree and recalculate, then another degree and so on till you see a pattern."

So having made a scale model (can't remember the scale now …say 1:3) on a large office desk using thick cardboard as the body, cross-member pivots and strut top mounting points, alloy strips for the struts and lower arms etc. and drawing pins in the pivot points, we rolled the model through its arc and it became evident we had NO roll centre containment at all (this is expressed these days as having 'Roll Centre Migration') in fact the lateral movement was enormous, down and way off the desk (outside of the bodywork) by metres if I remember correctly.

[All of this would of course be done via a CAD drawing these days but back when engineers used whatever they had to get a job done…]

So we scrambled to raise the inner lower arm pivot position on the cross member, lower the outer lower arm pivot position on the strut, and raise the steering rack position, including making its height adjustable to allow for bump-steer correction. Anyone who has done this will know it is not as easy as it sounds – so many snags and compromises to overcome.

Raising the steering rack the required amount meant it needed

Hard to see but a section of the trough cut out here.

to be where the collection trough for the dry sump pan was! And moving the inner pivots for the lower arms by the required amount meant they'd be a bit above the cross-member! Some very skilful fabrication by Pete made the resulting cross-member look not too unlike the original and Derro didn't seem to miss too much the piece he had to chop out of the dry sump pan.

After getting the roll centre problem resolved we were able to get back to something like 450lb springs in the front, which was where they should have been.

Testing thankfully showed our efforts were not in vain – the front immediately became responsive to spring, shock, and anti-roll bar rates and we were able to drop all of these dramatically.

I think the static ride height was raised a little to achieve the final 'sweet-spot'. Finally, the front spoiler height was adjusted down and fitted with a honeycomb under tray.

Jamie did all the Bilstein shock re-valveing, dyno testing, graphing and pairing in-house. Before the work to fix the roll centre he'd been struggling to get the spring rebound under control. It must have been a relief for him to be dealing with the much softer springs we ended up with. We made significant gains with shock re-valveing, particularly on the slow shaft speed setting. With all the rally experience he'd gained, Jamie had become a master in this field.

We then had very little remaining time to have both cars updated, spares machined/fabricated for the first race in 1982."

But now what to do with the rear semi-trailing arm, independent rear end, as this too had proven to have severe shortcomings?"

All of this work on the front roll centre was done without input from HM.

Modifications to the rear suspension came a bit later in the year.

BODYWORK

George Smith continues regarding modification work to the Bluebird body:

"As allowed wheel sizes grew during the Bluebird program we had to have three separate goes at accommodating these bigger and bigger wheel/tyres inside the wheel housings. I can still recall Dennis and Peter Thorn 'massaging' the wheel houses with heat and Indy hammer!

The roll cages were beautiful aluminium bolt-ins fabricated in-house by Pete Anderson.

There were no on-board air jacks back then, just 3mm alloy jacking platforms bolted to the front and rear of the sills where hand-held air bellows jacks were positioned by the wheel changers, with 'knocky gun' in the other hand and already attacking the first nut!

There were several fabricated and body-welded mountings here and there."

Regarding the wheel arch cutouts and fibreglass flairs, George says...

Some early body work, preparing for the fibreglass flares. Note coil over shocks ready to go in.

"Oh boy, those flairs – I reckon we were at about Mk 10 by the end of 1984 when the program wound up. They kept getting wider and wider. Harry Firth became a CAMS Technical Officer in the early 1980s – with him on one side of the car with tape measure in hand, and one of us on the other side of the car, we always managed to come in 1mm under the required width. Amazing!

McArthur Fibreglass in Keysborough was our go-to for all manufacture and upgrade of fibreglass components, their expertise seemed limitless and their workmanship second to none."

And then Den continues regarding the rear spoiler:

"Following a discussion with Jamie in which he said something like: George and Fred tell me we need more down force on the rear and my indicator markers on the rear shocks back this up. We need a spoiler similar to the Commodore.

"I went to see Neil McArthur[2] and asked if we could purchase a rear Commodore spoiler, which we did, and I brought it back to Healey road and fitted it up then made modifications to make it conform with the Bluebird shape. I took it back to Neil and asked him to make three-piece moulds and produce a part, which he did."

"We had it fitted up on a car and when HM came in, his eyes popped and he exclaimed... get that off there now...!"

Neither Den nor George can remember how we managed to get it approved for use but they agree that maybe we got HM to allow us to fit it in a testing session to see what difference it made. Maybe George Fury had a say in it, or Fred suggested it might be a good thing.

Sorry, a scan of a Polaroid: Rear spoiler in development.

The cars contained a lot of beautiful aluminium and steel fabrication by Pete Anderson and George Smith, true artists in my opinion, not the least of which confronted the observer when the boot lid was raised. The magnificent dry-break refuelling system together with the dry sump tank (at left) is my favourite – it weighs next to nothing and could cope with big guys slamming 40 litre fuel churns into them.

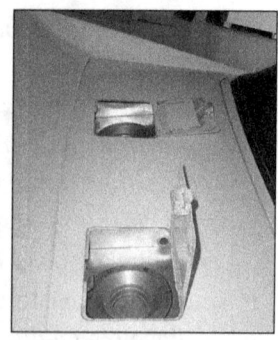

Flaps in boot lid held closed with magnets and flipped up to insert fuel filler and overflow churns.

---

2   ...who was also producing the Commodore spoilers.

REAR SUSPENSION

Peter Anderson remembered the evolution of the Bluebird's rear suspension so in his words:

"Derro, you may remember we were trying to get some better geometry in the rear with many alterations to pivot points on the rear cross member – I think at least six iterations of ear (mounting point) changes to the pivots for the A-arms but with little success.

In desperation Jamie and I worked on an alternative solution that would fit within the rules – suspension links could be added, provided the original pivots were still used. So I came up with the idea of fitting a pair of transverse links behind the drive shafts. These were mounted to upper and lower 'ears' welded to the rear of the A-arms and, for the inside, to a steel mounting frame bolted to the back of the diff housing. The original outer front A-arm mounting to

Spring seats and bump rubbers were not used. Coil over shocks instead.

Bushes removed from inner pivots so they became ineffective.

A standard independent rear suspension with semi-trailing arms.

Mounting ears for the outer end of the transverse links were welded to the top and bottom of the A arms.

The inner mounts for the transverse links and the strengthening brace. The diff cooler has been removed to show the top mount.

the cross member was retained using a rose joint but for the inner mounting, while still retaining the through bolt, we removed the bush in the arm, making this pivot no longer effective. It almost complied with the letter of the rules though!

This first attempt was not completely satisfactory as the inner mount steel frame cracked, so I then developed the idea of using two 8mm aluminium plates, one sandwiched between the diff and diff's rear cover, the other bolted to the back of the diff cover and picking up the rear diff mount to the body. These had eight holes per side allowing the inner rose joints a variety of mounting holes.

Due to the side loads imposed on the diff with this setup I made a 'V'-shaped diagonal brace from 4130 tube to brace the bottom centre of the rear aluminium plate to the rear subframe. This final arrangement proved to work really well.

I guess the first attempt (steel frame) ended up on our 'Trophy Shelf for Unsuccessful and Failed Parts'."

Once again, all the work to correct the problems with the rear roll centre was done in-house without input from management.

Our suspension modifications may have bent the rules (just like all the other serious Group C cars I'd suggest) but Howard and Fred offered no objection or obstruction to our efforts in this area and were in fact actively encouraging.

GEARBOX

George Smith continues:

"A Nissan FS5C71B carried over from Datsun Rallying as used in the standard 260Z but with Works Option 1 (direct 5th)ratio set.

This was the 71 Series box (distance in millimetres between main and countershaft centrelines) 'C' indicating Porsche, band type synchros, 'B' indicating the later 2-piece housing, Option 1, 5 speed ratios which provided a 1st gear adequate for launch and 1:1 top gear.

After a breakage of the input gear in the #56 Bluebird at the 1981 James Hardie 1000 at Bathurst, we had beefier versions made by Hollinger Engineering and this made the gearbox reliable until the seventh round of the ATCC in 1982 where we discovered the next weakest component – the second/third gear synchro hub (which transferred drive from countershaft to mainshaft for second or third gear.) This same component failed in car #15 at Bathurst in '83.

We considered the overall design and several components were robust enough to continue with so we commissioned Peter Hollinger to manufacture mainshaft, full sets of gears, selectors and dog-drive engagement rings.

Great work from Hollinger Engineering saw the problem solved and the gearbox bulletproof from then on.

Synchromesh vs. Dog engagement. A similar shaped engagement ring meshes with these dogs (on right) to lock the gear to the main shaft.

Footnote: From memory a stock ratio overdrive transmission was also on our homologation paperwork but we don't remember it ever being tested."

FINAL DRIVE (DIFFERENTIAL) ASSY

More from George Smith:

The Bluebirds used an R180 differential from the Datsun 6-cylinder range of cars of the era. Initially we ran with a 'CIG locker' (spider gears welded thereby removing the differential function), and soon after with machined 'spools' replacing spider gears and housing. These were bullet proof and greatly reduced the spinning mass inside the diff housing. I don't think we ever tested or raced with an LSD (Limited Slip Differential).

There was a wide selection of ratios to choose from, ranging between 3.7:1 and 5.4:1 – we'd select whichever best suited the circuit."

A differential allows drive wheels to turn at different speeds, a spool locks them together.

The R180 proved pretty reliable until its greatest test – the 1984 Bathurst race when a mêlée at the start required a restart and, as it turned out, three extra clutch dumps due to George's slightly muffed second start. The crown wheel and pinion failed on lap 80.

Somewhere quite early in the Bluebird program we broke a universal joint in a rear half shaft which led George S. to source a much more durable CV joint to replace them. He approached Alan Hamilton (the Australian Porsche distributor and a racing contact) who recommended and supplied us with Porsche CV joints, which were also in use in Formula 5000 race cars at the time. These proved completely reliable through to the end of the Bluebird program.

BRAKES

Front: Girling 4-piece alloy 4-Piston 1.75" open back, external hard line. Pads DS11 or 2451

Rear: Girling 1-piece alloy 4-Piston 1.5" open back, Pads DS11 or 2451

From memory we used 13" diameter by 1" thick front rotors and .75" thick on the rear.

Standard pendulum pedal assembly with driver cable adjustable balance bar utilizing the headlamp switch as the adjuster knob! See

DEVELOPMENT – BRAKES, WHEELS & TYRES

photo and white marker on the side of the shaft to allow turns to be counted.

We encountered very few problems with the whole braking system over the program.

Bathurst 1984 saw one major upgrade of the front brakes to eliminate a pad change during the race. We fitted twin calipers on the front, see photo, and upsized the front master cylinder to suit. This spec was carried through to the end of the Program.

The original front brake setup and the twin caliper setup we used for the '84 Endurance series.

WHEELS AND TYRES

Symmons 3-piece wheels were used and the inner and outer rims were changed as rim widths were steadily increased over the Group C racing life of the Bluebirds and wheel diameter increased from 15" to 16".

George Smith regarding the tyres: *Apart from some Good Years we tried once or twice early and then the Avons we ran from February 1984, Dunlops were what the Bluebirds mostly raced on. Russell Stuckey was the go to man for Dunlop race and rally tyres at the time and we'd built a*

great relationship with him over the years. Dunlop conventional belted (cross-ply) tyres were used for approximately 70% of our races but then, as radial belted tyres became de rigueur in 1984, we switched to Avon radials beginning at the Australian Touring Car Championship round at Sandown. It seemed a shame to move on from Stuckey san (it's funny how these nick-names stick) but Andy (Avon) McIntyre and Rowan Harman were good guys and we had some fun times with them too.

Your author swaps a Good Year cross-ply here at a pitstop at the '82 AEC at Surfers.

George remembers with a grin:

"Amazing, I remember the compound numbers of the Conventional Dunlop's we used:

The harder was 021, the softer, 095.

The reason I've remembered this was the way HRM used to pronounce them. We always wanted to use the softer one so that, when it was time to ask him, 'what compound are we going to start the race on Howard?' He would reply in his proper English tongue to our great delight and hidden mirth, "95 please George." but phonetically sounding like – "NEINTY FAVE." Whenever I hear that number anywhere to this day, I think back to those times with great delight."

We remember being somewhat surprised at the big difference in camber settings we needed to make the car work with the radials. We went from something like .75 to 1.5 degrees front camber with the conventionals and about zero on the rear, to the 5-6 degrees on the front and 2-3 degrees on the rear when we changed to radials."

1984 pole was with Avon radials.

ENGINE AND TURBOCHARGER

Powering the Bluebird Turbo was a Z18ET, 1770cc, 4-cylinder, single overhead camshaft motor that, apart from the cylinder head, was very similar to the L18 motor we'd used for years for rallying. Bore and stroke were 85 x 78mm as per a standard L18 in a 180B for instance. It used major components, most notably crankshaft and connecting rods, long tested in our years of rallying. Custom made forged pistons reduced the compression ratio to 6.7:1.

The aluminium cylinder head had two rocker shafts, mounted a little higher than the camshaft, and rocker arms which, activated by the camshaft, opened the valves. The camshaft was driven by a double-row chain from the crank, this mechanism nearly identical to the single cam L-series engines.

Somewhat interesting was the use of dual spark plugs but while this sounded slightly exotic it was actually an emission control strategy, seeking a more thorough burn in the combustion chamber. We continued to use this system thinking it more likely to assist performance than harm it. I remember removing the plug leads from one side then the other on the dyno one day – it didn't make too much difference.

The Z18ET used a Nissan version of the Bosch L-jetronic fuel injection and engine management system that utilised measured airflow and also throttle position to base its calculation for injector opening duration. This system and its components received a lot of my day and night mental activity for the three years we developed the car. A digital exhaust gas temperature read out was situated on the dash and the driver had access to a rheostat that tapped into the electronic control unit that was installed to affect injector duration. This proved to be only a minor tweak and of limited value, especially during the period we were running 100% duty cycle on the injectors without being aware.

My engine room at Healey Road.

At Bathurst in 1981, boost pressure was set and closely monitored by the Japanese engineers. Hasemi/Hoshino in car #56 were allowed 1.2 bar for qualifying (or so we were told) and this got them to 34th position on the grid. Gibson, driving car #55, could only have 1.1 bar, and with that Fred managed 43rd fastest.

To control boost levels on the original setup there was a 'wastegate' consisting of a flapper valve in the turbine housing which was actuated by an adjustable rod to a pressure diaphragm (see photos). The valve would allow exhaust gas to bypass the turbine, effectively slowing it. Making an adjustment when things were hot was fraught as I'd fumble in a very confined hot space with two 10mm spanners held in thick asbestos gloves and we battled with this setup until around mid 1982.

Original OEM turbocharger with integrated wastegate.

The standard engine also controlled inlet manifold pressure with an over-pressure blow-off valve screwed into the manifold. The Japanese engineers must have known these were problematic as they brought out a bag of different rated valves and also some blanking plugs, presumably in case none of the options would do the job. I gather none of them did as, by the end of practice, both cars were using the plug. From what I could gather, none of the valves could be made to release pressure gradually but would dump it suddenly – very disconcerting for drivers. We never went back to the relief valve.

Early in 1982 we received an evolution setup from Japan which included a more substantial wastegate unit which was integrated with an upgraded exhaust manifold. This and a new turbine housing had been cast from a high temperature steel named inconel. Apart from improvements in metallurgy, internal components of the turbocharger were unchanged.

This new wastegate setup had the facility of being able to provide a boost pressure connection, via a regulator, to the top of the actuator diaphragm to counteract the pressure beneath it and thereby enable the boost to be varied remotely. Without fully realising though initially, we were by this time, pretty much running the maximum boost the turbo could provide, making the wastegate almost redundant and this, naturally enough, was leading to turbines over-speeding and flying apart.

Turbochargers of this time mostly used fully floating bushes, with quite generous clearances, rather than ball bearings for the shaft connecting turbine to compressor. They relied on engine oil from the main gallery to keep everything centralised in the housings, to absorb pressure wave shocks, and also to help cool the cast iron bearing housing.

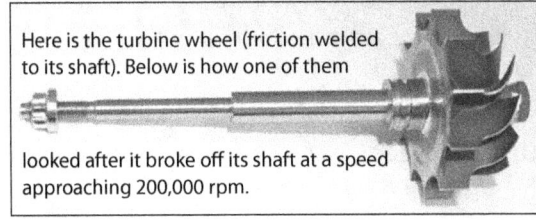

Here is the turbine wheel (friction welded to its shaft). Below is how one of them looked after it broke off its shaft at a speed approaching 200,000 rpm.

Every time a turbine suffered catastrophic failure bits and pieces of hi-temp steel, cast iron and sometimes a mangled bearing and a turbine oil seal would empty into the engine's oil sump necessitating a fairly major clean-up job. We developed a series of strainers and magnets to help manage this. I didn't keep score but apparently someone did and it was reported in the motoring media at one time that we had destroyed 44 turbochargers. Others have told me the number was actually higher than this.

The compressor wheel, attached at the other end of the shaft was usually not badly damaged in a blow up.

Somewhere amongst all this head scratching we had electronics boffin/friend, John Bailey develop for us a device to measure the speed of the turbocharger while running under power on the engine dynamometer. Things became clearer when I saw that the turbocharger speed was surging to exceed 200,000rpm! Compressor flow maps showed that this was way outside the band of speed where the unit could pump efficiently and probably meant it was operating at a terminal speed and likely cavitating – which was actually confirmed when a turbine wheel was forensically examined and showed the characteristic surface pitting.

Typically a blade or blades from the steel turbine wheel would detach causing sudden and severe out-of-balance and the wheel would break off its shaft. This, at very high speed, caused catastrophic destruction to at least the turbine and often to the whole turbocharger.

On the afore-mentioned 'Trophy Shelf for Unsuccessful and Failed Parts', in our morning tea break area, were a couple of the more dramatic examples of exploded turbine housings with turbine wheels forever lodged in the turbine outlet at weird angles.

The progression from using the OEM T3 Garrett turbocharger (hand-grenade), was made in several steps, which I'll detail soon. Some background though:

The power produced by an engine is determined by the volume and density of air/fuel mixture that it can be made to consume. So it slowly became clear to us that there was really only one significant way we were going to get past the frustration of non-competitiveness and smoky retirements. The turbo needed to pump more air.

Here, for readers who may be interested, is a short technical explanation of the turbocharger's function from Wikipedia:

"In naturally aspirated piston engines, intake gases are drawn or 'pushed' into the engine by atmospheric pressure filling the volumetric void caused by the downward stroke of the piston (which creates a low-pressure area), similar to drawing liquid using a syringe. The amount of air actually drawn in, compared with the theoretical amount if the engine could maintain atmospheric pressure, is called volumetric efficiency. The objective of a turbocharger is to improve an engine's volumetric efficiency by increasing the pressure of the intake gas (usually air) allowing more power per engine cycle.

The turbocharger's compressor draws in ambient air and compresses it before it enters into the intake manifold at increased pressure. This results in a greater mass of air entering the cylinders on each intake stroke. The power needed to spin the centrifugal compressor is derived from the kinetic energy of the engine's exhaust gases.

In automotive applications, 'boost' refers to the amount by which intake manifold pressure exceeds atmospheric pressure at sea level. This is representative of the extra air pressure that is achieved over what would be achieved without the forced induction. The level of boost may be shown on a pressure gauge, usually in bar, psi or possibly kPa. The control of turbocharger boost has changed dramatically over the 100-plus years of their use and modern turbo

DEVELOPMENT – ENGINE & TURBOCHARGER

The standard engine from the road-going Bluebird we began with in the racecar for initial testing at Calder. Note that there is no intercooler here – gas comes directly from compressor to inlet manifold. Note too the over-pressure blow off valve in the inlet manifold.

The race engine installed in BB1 for Bathurst. Note that the blow-off valve is still in use (abandoned later in practice) and that charge air now comes to the inlet manifold via the intercooler, which at that time was mounted underneath the radiator. The Japanese liked to use foam rubber to manage under-bonnet airflow!

An engine in C.1982 spec. showing the evolution exhaust manifold with provision for an external wastegate.

A T04 Garrett turbocharger bolted up to my dyno testing engine mid 1983 (note re-drilled turbine mounting flange). The difference to the sound and feel of the engine on the dynomometer was appreciable to say nothing of the increase in power.

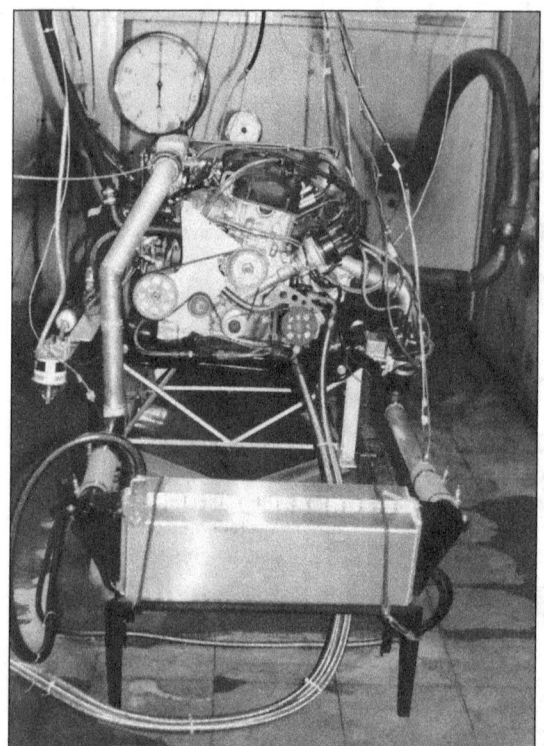

I think inspired by Barry Bray's success with a Lucas mechanical injection system on his Datsun Sports Sedan engine, we went to quite a bit of trouble to mount up this Kugelfischer forced induction, mechanical fuel injection pump and ancillaries to test, maybe late in 1982. The results were rather disappointing though and it was obvious considerably more work was required to produce a better 3D 'ramp' (called a spud) to get a driveable mixture progression. It was abandoned and we changed direction. Note the Pete-made air to water intercooler we used at the dyno.

This is the sister engine to the one George Fury used to set his famous Bathurst lap record. We took two new and identical engines for Car #15 to Bathurst in 1984 – this one didn't get a run. Note the brand new Graham Facey-made, polished stainless steel exhaust headers.

systems might use wastegates, blow-off valves, variable geometry or a combinations of these.

In petrol engine turbocharger applications, boost pressure is limited to keep the entire engine system, including the turbocharger, inside its thermal and mechanical design operating range. Over-boosting an engine frequently causes damage to the engine in a variety of ways including pre-ignition, overheating, and over-stressing the engine's internal hardware. For example, to avoid engine knocking (also known as detonation) and the related physical damage to the engine, the intake manifold pressure must not get too high, thus the pressure at the intake manifold of the engine must be controlled by some means. Opening the wastegate allows the excess energy destined for the turbine to bypass it and pass directly to the exhaust pipe, thereby reducing boost pressure. The wastegate can be either controlled manually (frequently seen in aircraft) or by an actuator (in very modern automotive applications, it is often controlled by the engine control unit)." There is considerably more technical information on turbochargers at Wikipedia.org.

Harking back to my earlier study of compressor flow maps I began contemplating how we might be able to come up with a turbocharger compressor that could pump more air at a slower shaft speed.

There were, it eventuated, 'high-flow' compressor wheels available and so with the help of Geoff Watson from Turbo Dynamics, we obtained supply and these gave us a little of what was required. Geoff also began balancing our turbo components to a higher standard. Grinding out and polishing the scroll inside the compressor was tried (a cow of a job for no apparent gain – I only did one). Later we attempted running closer wheel to housing tolerances and we discovered the limits of that strategy when wheel 'rubbing' caused grief.

Later again Geoff suggested we could try grinding down wheels from a T04 Garrett to fit our T3 housings and this gave us another incremental improvement. It had been this series of small improvements that had allowed us to remain in touch with the RX-7s and V8s during 1983 and early '84 but we also had many failures as we flirted with the T3s limits.

Other than a brief flirtation with an IHI turbocharger unit of similar specification in mid to late 1983 (described earlier), we ran this assembly through to mid 1984.

I had run an engine on the dynamometer with a T04 turbocharger and seen, felt and heard the difference it made, going from something that felt strangled, barely capable of 350bhp to a deeper sounding beast that could deliver 500bhp with the promise of more if required. It turned out there was no substitute for a larger compressor housing! I knew this was indeed where we needed to get to.

When I presented the evidence, HM dismissed it out of hand, he repeated the suggestion to raise the compression ratio and back off the boost. I knew exactly what that would achieve and, with my workmates' support, we chose a different path.

Geoff Watson, came up with the idea that, if CAMS could be convinced to allow us the freedom to upgrade our turbocharger while still complying with the homologated compressor inlet and turbine outlet sizes, he could sleeve back the T04 housings and grind the wheels to fit them. We thought that CAMS might be more inclined to be sympathetic if we could point to the fact that these two important sizes, nominated in our homologation papers, and easily accessible for checking, could be shown to be in use. This gave CAMS two measurements to check at scrutineering – and they allowed it!

In my mind this idea saved the whole Bluebird program.

Such was our team's intention and determination, it felt as though HM had little say in this progression. In hindsight I suspect he could already see his exit from the company and the team's handover to Fred. It felt like the team's leadership was based within the workshop during those last few months.

I thank my lucky stars there was sufficient time left before our last Bathurst, and that Howard had sufficient remaining faith in us, to play whatever part he did with CAMS in having them allow us this concession or we'd have been looking back at our Bluebird years as a disappointment.

The hybrid turbocharger we developed and took to Bathurst with CAMS's approval in 1984, gave us confidence the car would be able to run all day at the pointy end of the field if all else held together. What a shame events conspired to cause the diff to let us down.

For our first year, engines for both cars were built and tested in Japan and arrived before Bathurst in crates – approximately six of them! These kept us going for much of the four-year program, although I spent a lot of time inside every one of them! For Bathurst 1984 I built two brand new engines using new blocks, pistons and cylinder heads and used, but thoroughly checked, crankshafts and rods.

Apart from a period of drama with head gaskets, head studs, a cracked block and burned pistons during the first half of the Endurance Championship in 1984, much of which I think was due to detonation, the engine itself was pretty robust and reliable – most under bonnet catastrophes were caused by the turbocharger and its ancillaries.

Fred Gibson's published claim that our engines were only good for one qualifying lap and then trashed, is fanciful. We took two new engines to Bathurst in 1984 intending to use one for practice and qualifying, the other for the race. After his triumphant qualifying, when it came time to swap engines, George F said, *"this engine feels really good, I think we should leave it in."* It went on to do 146 laps in the race and was still powering the car through to the end of its career at Baskerville that year.

Never having been started until the mid naughties, the sister engine is now powering the restored BB2.

In Fred's defence, he had retired from driving at the end of 1983, the second half of which had been our most difficult period.

By far the most consuming part of my role as engine man with the team for these years was not so much working inside these engines but instead with most of the components attached externally.

After the first few turbine failures we looked into the effect, causes and mitigation of air pulse waves in the inlet tract as the throttle was continually opened and slammed shut, which was interesting at the time but didn't produce any improvements.

Once we'd overcome the handing problems with the car, the turbocharger was identified as our weakest link and it came under intense scrutiny as you'd expect. I had begun studying compressor flow maps which show the shaft speed, outlet air pressure, temperature and the flow rate for a specific air pump. Part of me knew this was the nub of our challenge but with HM slamming the lid on the possibility of using any other turbocharger I took my eye off that ball and we proceeded down a rocky path.

The thought that 'the output of the engine was fundamentally linked to the amount of fuel it could be made to burn' kept haunting me.

BMW were running a turboed engine with limited success and reliability in Formula 1 at the time so I digested everything I could find on their efforts. I was troubled by the size of the turbo components used on the 1600cc BMW engine – the compressor was huge compared to the one we were running while the turbine appeared to be of similar size to ours.

We battled on but it was another year before the penny completely dropped and our focus narrowed to 'how to pump more air'.

Along the way we'd discovered several other important and related issues, including the critical need to keep exhaust gas temperature under control.

This meant that the air/fuel mixture had to be properly controlled and those efforts led to a fuller understanding of the workings of the airflow meter, the injectors and the control computer (ECU). We even tried a Kugelfischer mechanical fuel injection system on the dyno (see photo page 172) albeit with fairly disappointing results.

Then, with my dyno engine increasingly bristling with temperature and pressure probes, I discovered early in 1983 that we had a significant pressure drop across the Japanese intercooler we'd been running[3]. This led to us tracking down a unit with a much larger frontal area, something that gave us a significant lift in air density and therefore power.

Some initiatives we made along the way produced astounding results, others were disappointing – I suppose that's the nature of development. The intercooler development was a good example. The road-going Turbo Bluebird managed without one for its 150-odd horsepower. The one the Japanese brought to Australia was approximately 150mm tall x 100mm deep x 500mm long and it sat beneath the radiator. Too many months later we discovered its inefficiency and its replacement, discovered by George Smith in an American catalogue, produced a significant gain.

It arrived as a core only so Pete Anderson fabricated and welded

---

[3] Boost pressure measured before the intercooler was quite a bit higher than when measured at the inlet manifold.

on end tanks for it and we immediately had near zero pressure loss and much better temperature reduction. To Fred Gibson's dismay, George bought another five more cores and Pete made up another five sets of end tanks, one for each of the three cars plus a spare for each! They made a very impressive pile in the workshop when completed!

Pete and George came up with a dastardly plan to further improve the charge density by spraying the contents of the on-board fire extinguisher through the intercooler on qualifying laps, which we tested with good results at the 1984 Sandown AEC round, and then took to Bathurst. Qualifying day there turned out to be the coldest on record and it wasn't really needed.

Speaking of such, in early 1982 we had our first sign that engine cooling was marginal on hot days and then at Bathurst that year the engine in #55 overheated and blew a head gasket. George Smith once again managed to track down a really nice cross-flow aluminium, Porsche 928 radiator with crimped on plastic tanks. These had inconvenient outlets so Pete removed them and again made beautiful, weld-on ones and we ended up with another impressive and expensive pile.

Pete pressing dimples into one of the end tanks and Derek caught admiring the result.

George folded up some aluminium duct-work to exhaust the intercooler's extracted heat underneath the new radiator and this all worked a treat.

Also quite early on we discovered, at a chassis dyno session, that the air filter we were using was causing a pressure drop to the inlet of the compressor — the place you least want to be causing a restriction. A fairly simple replacement produced a noticeable power increase. Thanks Wayne Manken. A little later we

discovered our replacement was allowing fine sand through which was eroding the aluminium compressor wheel so there was a further revision to resolve this.

When I was studying the fuel injectors, John Bailey brought a small oscilloscope to the workshop one day. We discovered that the standard injectors we were using were reaching 100% duty cycle before we even got to maximum power. Sourcing larger capacity injectors also made a noticeable difference. At about this time we also introduced the much larger air-flow meter from a 300ZX.

The size of the turbine's dump pipe was enlarged two or three times over the program to reduce exhaust back pressure. Removing flow restrictions was the most significant contribution to engine development for a while.

Partway through the first half of '84 we were having head sealing problems. I think the Japanese engines we began with had 85mm Cooper rings[4] fitted inside 89mm head gaskets. This arrangement got us through the first couple of years but as we increased turbo boost trying to stay competitive with the Mazdas and V8s we began having troubles, particularly when we suffered detonation.[5]

I became paranoid about detonation from this time and set up something on the engine dyno to ensure I didn't miss it. A length of 8mm copper tube was attached to one of the engine mounting bolts and the other end was attached to a large metal funnel that I tied up just outside the door to the dyno room. Any pinging was loudly amplified so that the load could very quickly be dumped. I think this was a Les Collins suggestion and it worked a treat.

The major cause of the detonation we discovered, and one that required some fairly serious engineering to overcome was piston overheating. We'd tried having pistons made with reduced ring land to bore clearance and with their compression rings moved lower, then tried ceramic coating on the piston crowns (a newish innovation for large turbo diesel truck motors of the time) but none of this fully resolved the issue.

---

4   Stainless steel tubular rings designed to seal combustion chambers under arduous conditions.

5   When excessive cylinder pressure or a hot spot in the combustion chamber causes the gas to ignite prematurely causing maximum cylinder pressure to occur before a piston has reached its apogee. This causes radically raised cylinder pressures and is indicated by a 'ping' noise. This can be very destructive, particularly in an engine that is already 'highly strung'.

Barry Bray had heard about the idea from F1 (I think) of squirting oil on the underside of the pistons to cool them. This sounded like a top idea so after a round table discussion, Pete set about making some to suit our engine.

He began by milling flats inside the crankcase adjacent to each cylinder and right below the main oil gallery, then drilled and tapped holes into the gallery. He then milled up a set of aluminium nozzle blocks which, when in situ, would aim a jet of oil at the underside of the piston as it came past bottom dead centre. Small notches were required in the piston skirts to clear these at the bottom of their travel.

Oil would flow from the gallery, through the centre of a drilled 8mm button-head cap screw and out a side port drilled to line up with the drilling in the alloy squirter block. We decided we didn't want to sacrifice oil pressure at idle speed though, so Pete went to the further trouble of installing, inside the 8mm cap screw, a ball and spring held in with a 4mm cap screw, also centre drilled and countersunk to provide a seat for the ball. After some spring swapping and testing and when all done and installed, these worked a treat and our piston overheating problem was behind us.

We (well, Graham Facey) had a couple of goes at fabricating tubular exhaust manifolds, initially from mild steel but these would crack in fairly short order and his version 2.0 was made from 316 Stainless Steel. Pete Anderson went to his workshop and gave him a lesson in SS TIG welding which he took to like a duck to water. Version 2.0 was still in use at the end of the Group C program.

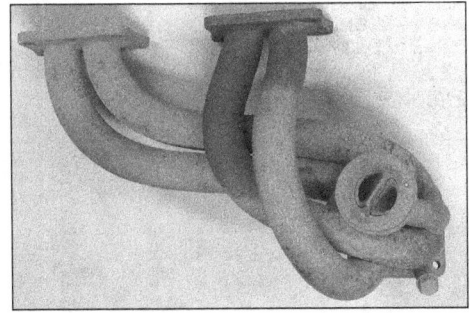

Version 1.0 in mild steel, cracked. See V2.0 on pg 174

It's difficult now to work out the exact order of problems surrounding this particular issue and the things we tried to resolve them but sometime before, in an attempt to keep the head sealed, I'd had studs made to replace the head bolts and at this time I felt the need to upgrade these. I deepened the bolt-holes in the block to give them more purchase and had studs and nuts made to suit from a tougher grade of steel (en35) and used better heat treating.

All this finally led me to discover that head studs (and other engine bolts) should stretch slightly when tensioned – it's this stretch that provides the 'clamp' effect and the tightening tension is specified to provide the required stretch and no more. Carefully sticking to the correct tension spec. is key though – before this realisation it was always very tempting to err on the side of 'just a bit more, with the thought that a bit more could only help. Not so – it's more a case of getting a good balance of strength with the right amount of stretch – stretching a bolt beyond it's ability to rebound can ruin the clamping effect as well as the bolt/stud.

At the 1983 Sandown Castrol 400 Fred DNF'd due to a cracked cylinder block through the thread hole for one of the centre studs (probably exacerbated by over-tensioning). Once we'd spied this when Fred pitted there was nothing for it but to put the car away for the day.

Another winning Bazza innovation was the stainless steel 'W' rings he came up with. These were to replace the Cooper rings we'd been using to seal the combustion chamber since the rally days. The 'W' rings were basically square section but had two concentric knife edged ridges on their top surface, the idea was that these would cut their own seal into the aluminium head surface. They sat in a step machined at the top of the cylinder bores, and were further supported by a head gasket made to suit an 89mm bore. These proved completely reliable for the rest of the Bluebird's program.

Versions I, II, III and IV of the exhaust dump pipes.

EXA Development

The engine that powered the Exa Turbo was the E15ET, a 1488cc (76mm × 82mm) single overhead camshaft version of the E-series which was the replacement for the long-running A-series. In standard configuration it would produce 85 kW or 113 bhp.

The camshaft was driven by toothed belt which also drove a jackshaft in the block, located where the OHV camshaft in the A-series lived, and this drove the oil pump as per the A-series.

Engine installed in the EXA and ready to fire up.

The cylinder head had a compact design with a single rocker shaft sitting directly above the camshaft. The distributor was driven directly from the end of the camshaft.

Bazza sourced a set of Carrillo con rods from the US, forged pistons were made locally by Special Piston Services, the crankshaft was fillet rolled, heat treated and balanced by Crankshaft Rebuilders. We tidied up the head and assembled it with inconel exhaust valves etc. Many of the lessons we'd learned from the Bluebird Turbo up until that time were of course rolled into this project so that, other than head sealing, it was mostly a reliable little power plant from the get go.

The head sealing issue was resolved at the end of 1983, straight after the AGP support race at Calder. We abandoned the solid copper gasket and Baz had engineer friend John Genat make a set of the stainless steel 'W' rings to fit the 76mm bore and I organised a custom

Building the dry sump pan on the E15 block

Showing fr brake, transmission cooling pump, turbocharger compressor (pumping straight into intercooler) and standard wastegate actuator.

head gasket with seal rings to go behind them. There were no more head gasket issues after that.

What really made the EXA a gun though was that there'd been a tiny stuff up with the homologation of the turbocharger. Original equipment was a T2 Garrett but the homologation papers read T3 – same as the Bluebird – which we knew was good for 350 bhp!

After the gearbox failed in its first race (the Castrol 400 at Sandown in 1983) Bazza took the gear set to Hollingers and had a better set of ratios made for the car and with dog engagement. This allowed for slightly wider gears as a bonus.

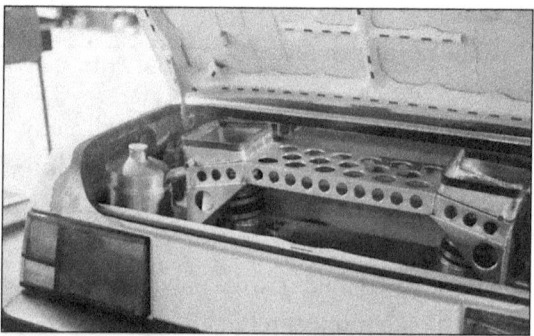

Another beautiful dry-break fuelling setup and oil tank.

Initially the racecar ran the standard drive shafts, the LH one approximately three time longer than the RH. When there was general agreement that this was the main cause of the rather drastic torque-steer, Baz set about engineering a fix.

He built an outrigger bearing housing mounted to the gearbox and a flanged shaft to run from that to the diff. He could then

The mould for the front fibreglass components.

use a second RH drive shaft from that bearing to the wheel hub. While not completely curing the torque-steer, this solution greatly improved the situation and the drivers only had to remember how bad it had originally been to feel better about driving it afterwards.

Out in the sunlight for the first time and ready for war paint. From some angles it was quite a smart looking car.

It was such a shame that the gearbox layshaft bearing collapsed in the EXA's last big test. Two weeks until the Australian Grand Prix meeting at Calder was just not enough time to engineer a solution to that problem and the pocket rocket didn't really get a chance to show how bright it could shine.

The little rocket ship appears eager to get going!

The EXA's first outing at Sandown. Author in gumboots on LH front, Den on LH rear, Wyn has a churn going down and Gator has another ready to go. Stevie has the overflow bottle and Fred checks in with Christine.

TECHNICAL ACKNOWLEGMENTS

I'd like to thank the businesses and people who supported me with engine development, machining work and component manufacture over these years.

Firstly, **Tom Sekeres**, a countryman of George Fury who introduced me to the engine dynomometer and the sensory overload of our engines running at full power, up close and personal. Tom was a great mentor for a young guy getting serious about competition engine tuning. Jamie, Les Collins and I bought his business when Tom wanted to retire. From then on I no longer had to make a booking!

Brian Berryman of Berryman Engines was innitially my go-to man for engine component machining and **Rick McQuaige** who at the time worked there, did a superb job on our cylinder heads for the last few years.

Ian Shugg of Crankshaft Rebuilders later took over machining work on engine blocks, crankshafts and rods.

John Patterson of Special Piston Services always made our pistons.

Jack Mayes built sand-bent steel exhaust headers until in 1984 **Graham Facey** took over and, after some coaching from Peter Anderson, built two superb polished stainless steel, sand-bent exhaust manifolds for us that, while improving performance by a small amount, vastly improved reliability and enhanced the under-the-bonnet appearance by light years.

John Bailey greatly assisted with all sorts of electronic challenges.

Geoff Watson of Turbo Dynamics powered our turbocharger development efforts and saved the day!

Tom and myself with Bazza's LZ race motor on the dyno.

ADDENDUM

The circuits we raced at:

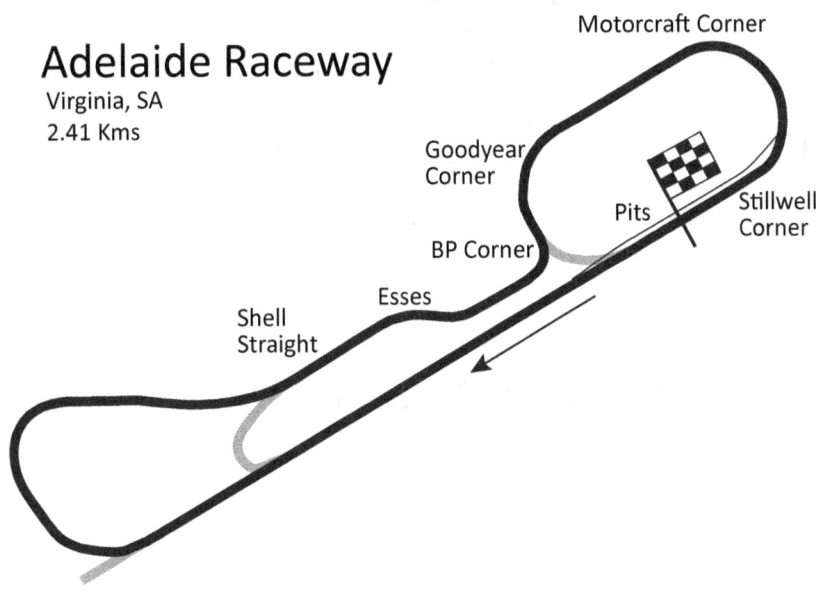

Adelaide Raceway
Virginia, SA
2.41 Kms

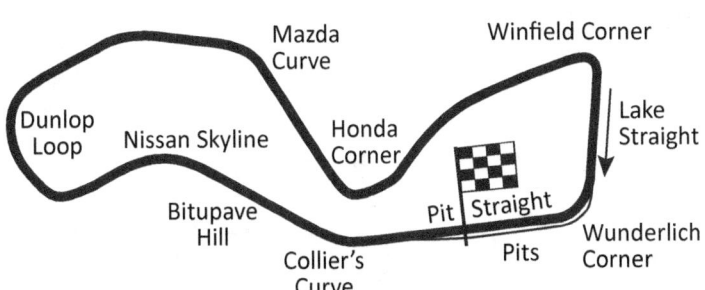

Amaroo Park Raceway
Annangrove NSW
1.94 Kms

Baskerville Raceway
Hobart TAS
2.01 Kms

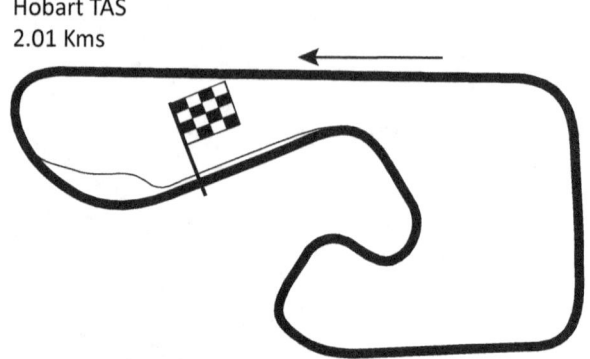

Calder Park Raceway
Keilor, VIC
1.609 Kms

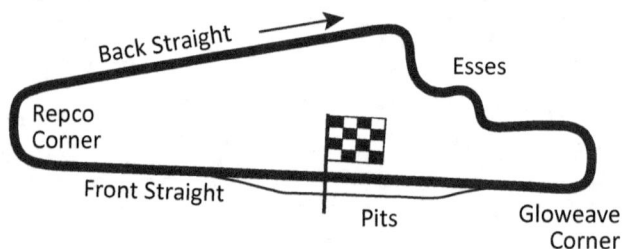

Lakeside Raceway
Kurwongbah QLD
2.41 Kms

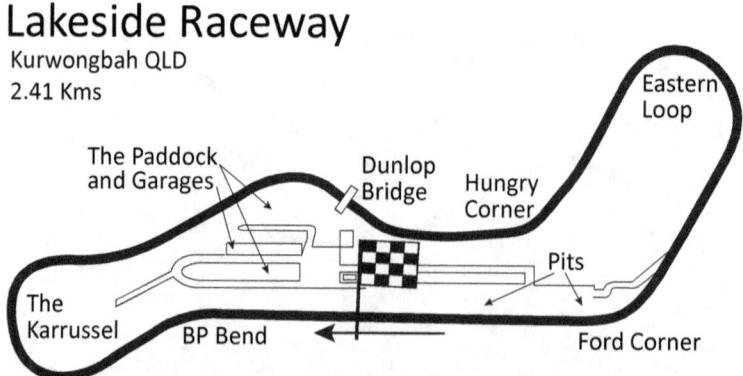

ADDENDUM

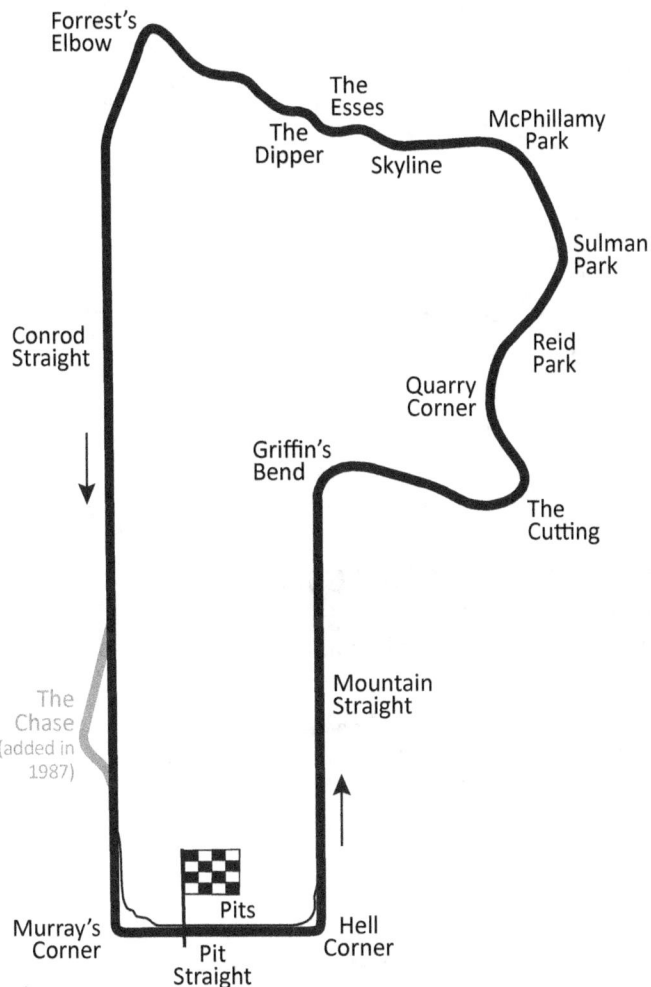

There's a comprehensive description including historical notes of this famous circuit at
https://en.wikipedia.org/wiki/Mount_Panorama_Circuit

Sandown Park Raceway
Melbourne VIC
3.10 Kms

- Rothmans Rise
- The Esses
- Goodyear Corner
- Arco Corner
- Pits
- Dunlop Bridge
- Shell Corner

Sandown Park Raceway
Melbourne VIC
3.88 Kms (post 1984 redevelopment)

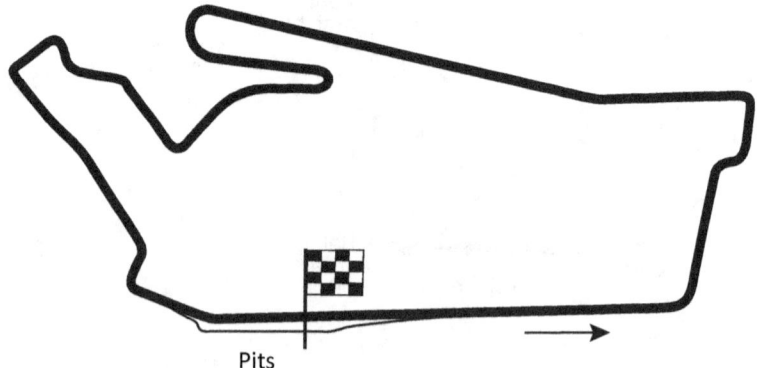

Pits

ADDENDUM

Surfers Paradise Raceway
Carara, Gold Coast, QLD
3.22 Kms

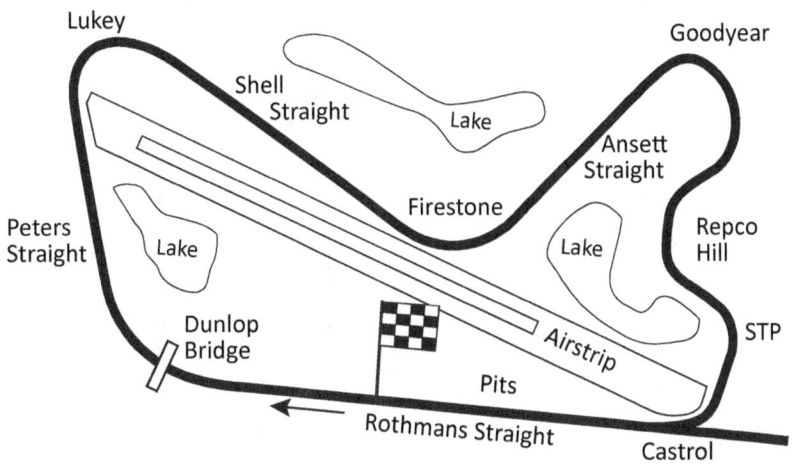

Symmons Plains Raceway
Launceston TAS
2.41 Kms

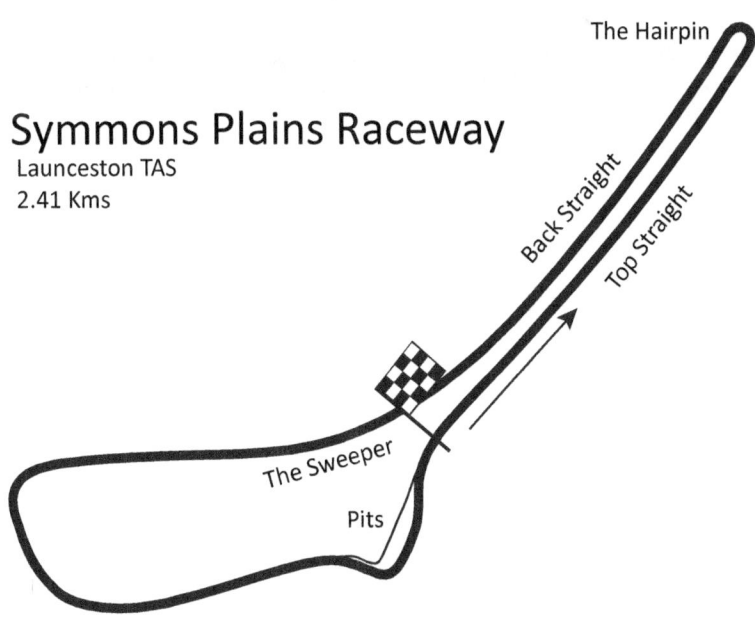

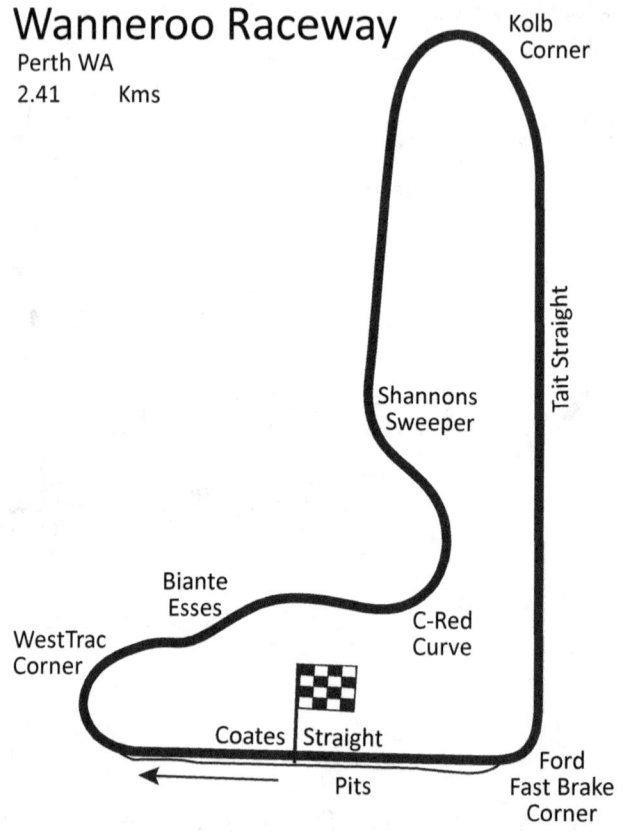

CAR HISTORY

Although Bluebirds 1 and 2 were completed simultaneously at our Braeside factory in 1981 as previously indicated I've chosen to name the one that came out from Japan nearly completed, BB1 and the car that was built up into a race car from a Bluebird Turbo road car at Braeside as BB2. Both first raced at the 1981 James Hardie 1000 at Bathurst and both survived in tact through to the end of the program in late 1984.

BB1 was Chassis no. P910-110136 and, as stated, arrived in Australia during late August 1981 as a near complete race car having been assembled in Japan including several major parts that had been fabricated in Australia and sent over.

It's racing history is as follows:

	Event	Driver/s	Grid pos'n	Result
1981	James Hardie 1000	Hasemi / Hoshino	31st	DNF (gearbox)
1982	ATCC Rnd 1 Sandown	F. Gibson (2 heats)	16th	12th & 11th
	AMSCAR Rnd 1 Amaroo	F. Gibson	7th	14th
	AMSCAR Rnd 2 Amaroo	F. Gibson	18th	7th
	AMSCAR Rnd 3 Amaroo	F. Gibson	8th	9th
	AMSCAR Rnd 4 Amaroo	F. Gibson	5th	12th
	CRC 300 Amaroo	F. Gibson	5th	2nd
	AEC Rnd 1 Oran Park	F. Gibson	11th	DNF (driveshaft)
	AEC Rnd 2 Sandown	F. Gibson	20th	8th
	James Hardie 1000	Hasemi / Hoshino	3rd	8th
	AEC Rnd 4 Surfers	F. Gibson	15th	6th
	AEC Rnd 5 Adelaide	F. Gibson	7th	4th
1983	AMSCAR Rnd 1 Amaroo	F. Gibson (3 heats)	1st	DNS (all)
	ATCC Rnd 1 Calder	F. Gibson	5th	7th
	AMSCAR Rnd 2 Amaroo	F. Gibson (3 heats)	3rd	DNS, 3rd, 4th
	ATCC Rnd 2 Sandown	F. Gibson	6th	DNF (overheat)
	AMSCAR Rnd 3 Amaroo	F. Gibson (3 heats)	3rd	2nd, 1st, 1st
	AMSCAR Rnd 4 Amaroo	F. Gibson (3 heats)	3rd	4th, 3rd, DNF (turbo)
	ATCC Rnd 7 Oran Park	F. Gibson	13th	10th
1984	AMSCAR Rnd 1 Amaroo	G. Scott (3 heats)	2nd	Last, 2nd, 2nd
	AMSCAR Rnd 2 Amaroo	G. Scott (3 heats)	1st	8th, 1st, 2nd
	AMSCAR Rnd 3 Amaroo	G. Scott (3 heats)	2nd	3rd, 3rd, DNF (turbo)
	AMSCAR Rnd 4 Amaroo	G. Scott (3 heats)	2nd	5th, 2nd, 1st
	AEC Rnd 1 Amaroo	G. Scott	1st	1st

BB2 was Chassis no. P910-109045 and was imported to Australia as a new evaluation Bluebird Turbo in late 1980. We began stripping it as time permitted early in 1981 in order to build a race car and it was completed mid September in time for some testing at Calder Park before being trailered to Bathurst. It's racing history is as follows:

	Event	Driver/s	Grid pos'n	Result
1981	James Hardie 1000 Bathurst	F. Gibson / G. Fury	43rd	DNF
	AEC Rnd 4 Surfers Paradise	G. Fury	14th	DNF
1982	ATCC Rnd 1 Sandown	G. Fury (2 heats)	13th	10th, DNF (overheat)
	ATCC Rnd 2 Calder	G. Fury	6th	2nd
	ATCC Rnd 7 Adelaide	G. Fury	6th	DNF
	AMSCAR Rnd 4 Amaroo	G. Fury	9th	10th
	CRC 300 Ammaroo	G. Fury	6th	DNF
	AEC Rnd 1 Oran Park	G. Fury	3rd	Mid-field
	AEC Rnd 2 Sandown	G. Fury	6th	DNF
	AEC Rnd 3 James Hardie 1000	G. Fury / F. Gibson	10th	DNF
	AEC Rnd 4 Surfers Paradise	G. Fury	3rd	2nd
	AEC Rnd 5 Adelaide	G. Fury	2nd	7th (strut top nut)
1983	ATCC Rnd 1 Calder	G. Fury	3rd	2nd
	ATCC Rnd 2 Sandown	G. Fury	2nd	4th
	ATCC Rnd 3 Symmons Plains	G. Fury	4th	3rd
	ATCC Rnd 4 Wanneroo	G. Fury	5th	2nd
	AMSCAR Rnd 4 Amaroo	C. Gibson (3 heats)	11th	?, 9th, 4th
	ATCC Rnd 5 Adelaide	G. Fury	2nd	3rd
	ATCC Rnd 6 Surfers Paradise	G. Fury	5th	4th
	ATCC Rnd 7 Oran Park	G. Fury	1st	5th
	AEC Rnd 1 Amaroo	G. Fury	3rd	1st
	AEC Rnd 3 Sandown	F. Gibson	15th	DNF
	AEC Rnd 4 James Hardie 1000	G. Fury / F. Gibson	16th	22nd
1984	ATCC Rnd 2 Symmons Plains	G. Fury	4th	DNF

BB3 was Chassis no. P910-110052 and was built at the Healey Road workshops from a brand new Japanese IRS body shell begun early 1983 and first raced August '83. It's racing history is as follows:

	Event	Driver/s	Grid pos'n	Result
1983	AEC Rnd 2 Oran Park	G. Fury	3rd	1st
	AEC Rnd 3 Sandown	G. Fury	5th	DNF (IHI turbo)
	AEC Rnd 4 James Hardie 1000	G. Fury / G. Scott	2nd	DNF
	AGP Support Calder	G. Fury	1st	1st
1984	ATCC Rnd 1 Sandown	G. Fury	5th	5th
	ATCC Rnd 3 Wanneroo	G. Fury	2nd	DNF (turbo)
	ATCC Rnd 5 Oran Park	G. Fury	5th	DNF (incident steering)
	ATCC Rnd 6 Lakeside	G. Fury	3rd	1st
	ATCC Rnd 7 Adelaide	G. Fury	1st	DNF (turbo)
	AEC Rnd 2 Oran Park	G. Fury	2nd	DNF (head gasket)
	AEC Rnd 3 Sandown	G. Fury	1st	DNF (turbo)
	AEC Rnd 4 James Hardie 1000	G. Fury / G. Scott	1st	16th
	AEC Rnd 5 Surfers	G. Scott	4th	DNF (incident steering)
	AGP Support Calder	G. Fury	1st	1st
	Baskerville Touring Car Cup	G. Seton	?	DNF (incident damage)

The **EXA Turbo** was Chassis no. KHN12-0000298 and was built at our Healey Road workshops in the middle of 1983 by Barry Bray with assistance from Ian Walburn and from myself with the engine. It first raced at Amaroo in July '83. It's racing history is as follows:

	Event	Driver/s	Grid pos'n	Result
1983	AEC Rnd 3 Castrol 400 Sandown	C. Gibson	25th	DNF (Gearbox)
	AEC Rnd 3 James Hardie 1000	C. Gibson / B. Muir	37th	DNF (Head gasket)
	AEC Rnd 4 Surfers Paradise	C. Gibson	1st (in class)	DNF (Head gasket)
1984	AMSCAR Rnd 1 Amaroo	C. Gibson (3 heats)	7th	8th, 9th, 7th
	AMSCAR Rnd 2 Amaroo	C. Gibson (2 heats)	9th	7th, DNF (crash)
	AMSCAR Rnd 3 Amaroo	C. Gibson (3 heats)	11th	?, ?, DNF (crash)
	AEC Rnd 1 Silastic 300 Amaroo	C. Gibson	?	DNF (crash)
	AEC Rnd 2 Oran Park 250	C. Gibson	?	
	AEC Rnd 4 James Hardie 1000	C. Gibson / G. Seton	26th	DNF (gearbox)

Post Nissan Sport, ownership of the cars is as follows:

BB1 was sold to Jarrett Nissan, a dealership in Adelaide, in 1985. Grant Jarrett raced it as a sports sedan at 36 meetings according to its log book, mostly in South Australia but also a few in Victoria between 1985 and 1992. In 1990 it was advertised for sale and was snapped up by Pete Anderson with the intention to preserve it and not allow it to be further degraded, as always happens when a car is raced in a category where there are no fixed technical specs and regulations.

Pete took a wall out of his workshop at his home on the Whitsunday Coast in Queensland to allow the car's storage inside and there it stayed until March 2017. The car was tracked down, and Pete was made an offer he couldn't refuse by Anthony Alford who, he discovered, was keen to have Gibson Motorsport faithfully restore it to its original Group C state as raced by Nissan. This job was completed in 2020 and it is hoped Alford will use it to compete in Historic Race meetings.

BB2 was sold to Bruce Peacock in WA late in 1984 (Bruce had been recommended to Howard by his uncle, Gordon Crump, the chief of Datsun Distribution in WA). Beginning in 1985 Bruce raced it in Sports Sedan Category 2 at Wanneroo Raceway and the car was also shipped to Malaysia where he raced it in a support race to the Selangor Grand Prix.

Early in 1987 the car was on-sold to Damon Russell Racing who competed with it at Wanneroo 1987 to 1990. During this time the engine was replaced with an FJ20 supplied by Gibson Motorsport after the Z18T block crank etc. were damaged (all parts were kept for possible future rebuild). From 1990 to 1998 Damon Russell Racing kept the car in storage.

In 1998 Bruce Peacock re-purchased with the intention to rebuild.

In 2003 it was sold to Paul Kramer, also in WA, but shortly after he sold it on, with all spares, to Adam Workman in NSW.

The car was slowly restored between 2003 & 2021 to its 1984 presentation and is now ready to race again in Group C Historic Racing category 5.

BB3 remained with Gibson Motorsport until 2002 but for 1985 it was leased to Queensland Nissan dealer Armstrong Nissan for Gary Scott to race as a sports sedan. In 2002 it was sold to Terry Ashwood who owned it until 2013 when Brian Henderson bought the car and has lovingly restored it to better than the condition when it first rolled out of the Healey Road workshop in 1983.

To the end of 2021 it had only been run once since its last race in 1985 with Gary Scott and that was at Sandown in November 2014.

It will soon be seen again on circuits running against its sister Bluebirds in Group C Historic races.

The EXA remained with Gibson Motorsport from 1985 until 2002 when it was sold to Terry Ashwood.

In 2006 it was onsold to Justin Nillson and remains in his possession. It too has undergone a loving restoration in recent years and will be competing with the Bluebirds in post COVID Historic Racing series.

Sandown 2016. Left to right: David Foster (mechanic), John French, Adam Workman (owner BB2), Peter Workman (dec), Colin Matherson (dec), Fred Gibson, Brian Henderson (owner BB3).

ADDENDUM

This is the spreadsheet (sans colour, sorry) I used to reconstruct the history of the cars, drivers and their races.

Year	Event	Car	Heat	Driver/s	Grid	Result	Notes
		BB1 (Jap)		Hasemi/Hoshino			
		BB2 (Oz)		Fury			
		BB3 (Oz)		Gibson			
		EXA		C. Gibson			
				Scott			
1981	James Hardie 1000 Bathurst - Oct 4	BB1 #56		Hasemi/Hoshino	31st	DNF	66 laps. Battery and gearbox
		BB2 #55		Gibson/Fury	43rd	DNF	30 laps. Broken rose joint
	AEC Rnd 4 Int'l Resort 300 Surfers – Nov 1	BB2 #55		Fury	14th	DNF	Broken Rr stub axle, lost wheel
1982	ATTC Rnd 1 Sandown - Feb 18	BB2 #55	H1	Fury	13th	10th	½ lap back
		BB2 #55	H2	Fury		DNF near end	Overheating – (overall 11th)
		BB1 #56	H1	Gibson	16th	12th	1+ lap down
		BB1 #56	H2	Gibson		11th	Lapped (overall 7th)
	ATTC Rnd 2 Calder - Feb 28	BB2 #55		Fury	6th	2rd	28 secs behind Johnson
	ATTC Rnd 3 Symmons Plains - Mar 7					Didn't go	
	AMSCAR Better Brakes Rnd 1- Mar 14	BB1 #56		Gibson	7th	14th	Wet, exciting race
	ATTC Rnd 4 Oran Park - Mar 21					Didn't go	
	ATTC Rnd 5 Lakeside - April 4					Didn't go	
	AMSCAR Rnd 2 - April 11	BB1 #56		Gibson	18th	7th	
	ATTC Rnd 6 Wanneroo - April 28					Didn't go	
	ATTC Rnd 7 Adelaide - May 2	BB2 #55		Fury	6th	DNF	Broke 3rd gear at start, retired on lap 18
	ATTC Rnd 8 Surfers - May 16					Didn't go	
	AMSCAR Rnd 3 - May 23	BB1 #56		Gibson	8th	9th	
	AMSCAR Rnd 4 - July 1	BB1 #56		Gibson	5th	12th	
		BB2 #55		Fury	9th	10th	
	CRC 300 Amaroo - Aug 8	BB1 #56		Gibson	5th	2nd	
		BB2 #55		Fury	6th	DNF	Taken out by Grice while in a strong second place
	AEC Rnd 1 Oran Park Sept 12	BB2 #55		Fury	3rd	Mid field	Boost leak, lost 8 laps, finished
		BB1 #56		Gibson	11th	DNF	Failure in drive line at start
	AEC Rnd 2 Castrol 400 Sandown - Sept 2	BB2 #55		Fury	6th	DNF	Got to 6th late in race but lost boost
		BB1 #56		Gibson	20-ish	8th	3 laps down
	AEC Rnd 3 JH 1000 Bathurst - Oct 3	BB1 #56		Hasemi/Hoshino	3rd	8th + class 1st	10 laps down
		BB2 #55		Fury/Gibson	10th	DNF	Only 40 of 163 laps completed - Head gasket
	AEC Rnd 4 GC 300 Surfers - Nov 7	BB2 #55		Fury	3rd	2nd	
		BB1 #56		Gibson	15th	6th	
	AEC Rnd 5 Nissan 300 Adelaide - Dec 5	BB2 #55		Fury	2nd	7th	Stripped thread on top of fr strut mid race
		BB1 #56		Gibson	7th	4th	
1983	AMSCAR Rnd 1 - March 6	BB1 #56	H1	Gibson	1st	DNS	Had pole position but didn't start - tailshaft fails
		BB1 #56	H2	Gibson	1st	DNS	Didn't start
		BB1 #56	H3	Gibson	1st	DNS	Didn't start
	ATTC Rnd 1 Calder - Feb 6	BB2 #55		Fury	3rd	2nd	By about 8 seconds. Very hot weekend
		BB1 #56		Gibson	5th	7th	>2 laps down
	ATTC Rnd 2 Sandown - Feb 20	BB2 #55		Fury	2nd	4th	Very close to 3rd
		BB1 #56		Gibson	6th	DNF	Holed radiator in contact with Carter stopped back strt
	ATTC Rnd 3 Symmons Plains - Mar 13	BB2 #55		Fury	4th	3rd	Handling issues
	AMSCAR Rnd 2 - April 10	BB1 #56	H1	Gibson	3rd	DNS	Had 3rd on grid but DNS - broken drive shaft
		BB1 #56	H2	Gibson	3rd	3rd	
		BB1 #56	H3	Gibson	3rd	4th	
	ATTC Rnd 4 Wanneroo - Apr 21	BB2 #55		Fury	5th	2nd	
	AMSCAR Rnd 3 - May 22	BB1 #56	H1	Gibson	3rd	2rd	
		BB1 #56	H2	Gibson	3rd	1st	
		BB1 #56	H3	Gibson	3rd	1st	Very wet
	AMSCAR Rnd 4 - July 10	BB1 #56	H1	Gibson	3rd	4th	
		BB2 #55	H1	C. Gibson	11th	?	
		BB1 #56	H2	Gibson	3rd	3rd	
		BB2 #55	H2	C. Gibson	11th	9th	
		BB1 #56	H3	Gibson	3rd	DNF	Turbo failure
		BB2 #55	H3	C. Gibson	11th	4th	

Year	Event	Car	Heat	Driver/s	Grid	Result	
1983	ATTC Rnd 5 Adelaide - May 1	BB2 #55		Fury	2nd	3rd	
	ATTC Rnd 6 Surfers - May 15	BB2 #55		Fury	5th	4th	
	ATTC Rnd 7 Oran Park - May 29	BB2 #55		Fury	1st	5th	
		BB1 #56		Gibson	13th	10th	
	ATTC Rnd 8 Lakeside - June 19				Didn't go		HM pulled the team
	AEC Rnd 1 Silastic 300 Amaroo Aug 7	BB2 #55		Fury	3rd	1st	By >1 lap to Brock
		BB1 #56		Gibson	7th	DNF	Claimed low boost and retired as Fury about to lap
	AEC Rnd 2 Oran Park 250 - Aug 21	BB3 #57		Fury	3rd	1st	First outing win for BB3
		BB1 #56		Gibson/Scott	5th	DNF	Blown turbo on last lap while running third
		BB2 #55		French		DNS	Crashed by Scott in practice
	AEC Rnd 3 Castrol 400 Sandown - Sept 11	BB3 #15		Fury	5th	DNF	Blown IHI turbo
		BB2 #16		Gibson	15th	DNF	Unknown
		Exa #60		C. Gibson	25th	DNF	Gearbox broke
	AEC Rnd 4 JH 1000 Bathurst - Oct 2	BB3 #15		Fury/Scott	2nd	DNF	Broke g'box end lap 1 then did another 130 laps
		BB2 #16		Gibson/French	16th	22nd	
		BB1 #T					Test car
		Exa #60		C. Gibson/Bob Muir	37th	DNF	Just 14 laps – Head gasket
	AEC Rnd 5 Surfers - Oct 30	Exa #60		C. Gibson	1st <3L	DNF	Bad mis-fire, retired lap 55 with a leaking head gasket
	Support race to AGP Calder – Nov 13	BB3 #15		Fury	1st	1st	Berri Fruit Juices 40 lapper
		Exa #60		C. Gibson	?	DNF	More overheating
	AEC Rnd 6 Nissan 300 Adelaide - Nov 20				Didn't go		
1984	ATTC Rnd 1 Sandown - Feb 18	BB3 #15		Fury	5th	5th	
	AMSCAR Rnd 1 - March 4	BB1 #16	H1	Scott	2nd	Last	After an off from a touch with Masterton
		Exa #60	H1	C. Gibson	7th	8th	
		BB1 #16	H2	Scott	2nd	2nd	
		Exa #60	H2	C. Gibson	7th	9th	
		BB1 #16	H3	Scott	2nd	2nd	
		Exa #60	H3	C. Gibson	7th	7th	
	ATTC Rnd 2 Symmons Plains - Mar 11	BB2 #15		Fury	4th	DNF	Broke a half shaft on start line. (BB3 had a miss)
	AMSCAR Rnd 2 - April 8	BB1 #16	H1	Scott	1st	8th	Punted off
		Exa #60	H1	C. Gibson	9th	7th	
		BB1 #16	H2	Scott	1st	1st	
		Exa #60	H2	C. Gibson	9th	DNF	Crashed
		BB1 #16	H3	Scott	1st	2nd	
		Exa #60	H3	C. Gibson	9th	DNS	Crash damage
	ATTC Rnd 3 Wanneroo - Apr 21	BB3 #15		Fury	2nd	DNF	Turbo fail at about one third distance
	ATTC Rnd 4 Surfers - May 13				DNS	DNS	Didn't go
	AMSCAR Rnd 3 - May 20	BB1 #16	H1	Scott	2nd	3rd	
		Exa #60	H1	C. Gibson	11th	?	
		BB1 #16	H2	Scott	2nd	3rd	
		Exa #60	H2	C. Gibson	11th	?	
		BB1 #16	H3	Scott	2nd	DNF	Blown turbo
		Exa #60	H3	C. Gibson	11th	DNF	Crash
	ATTC Rnd 5 Oran Park - May 27	BB3 #15		Fury	5th	DNF	Grice drove into Fury breaking steering Turn 3, Lap 1
	ATTC Rnd 6 Lakeside - June 17	BB3 #15		Fury	3rd	1st	Very wet (HM absent)
	ATTC Rnd 7 Adelaide - July 1	BB3 #15		Fury	1st	DNF	Failed turbo while leading well into race. Last turbo fail
		BB1 #16		Scott	7th	4th	
	AMSCAR Rnd 4 - July 8	BB1 #16	H1	Scott	2nd	5th	
		BB1 #16	H2	Scott	2nd	2nd	
		BB1 #16	H3	Scott	2nd	1st	
	AEC Rnd 1 Silastic 300 Amaroo Aug 5	BB1 #16		Scott	1st	1st	
		Exa #60		C. Gibson	?	DNF	Hit wall on pit straight
	AEC Rnd 2 Valvoline 250 Oran Park - Aug 19	BB3 #15		Fury	2nd	DNF	Head gasket fail lap 33
		Exa #60		C. Gibson	?	?	
	AEC Rnd 3 Castrol 500 Sandown - Sept 9	BB3 #15		Fury/Scott	1st	DNF	Cracked block
	AEC Rnd 4 JH 1000 Bathurst - Sept 30	BB3 #15		Fury/Scott	1st	16th	after a diff change – 146 laps
		Exa #16		C. Gibson/Seton	26th	DNF	76 laps Gearbox front layshaft bearing
	AEC Rnd 5 Motorcraft 300 Surfers - Nov 4	BB3 #16		Scott	4th	DNF	Bent steering from small collision with Moffat
	Support race to AGP Calder – Nov 13	BB3 #15		Fury	1st	1st	Berri Fruit Juices 40 lapper
	Baskerville Touring Car Cup – 25 November	BB3 #15		G. Seton		DNF	Race incident with Steve Harrington's Commodore

PERSONAL THANKS

I wish to thank particularly George Smith but also Pete Anderson, Brian Henderson and Adam Workman (two of the cars' current owners) who have helped immensely with research into the history told here, as well as contributed narrative that I've been able to quote and photos that I've included. Contributions have also been made by George Fury, Gary Scott, Roger Bonhomme, Den Watson and Barry Bray.

Thank you too to Aaron Noonan of AN1 Media who provided valuable advice regarding the use of many of the images in this book.

I also wish to thank the late Jamie Drummond as it was he who gave me the shove to begin this project, saying, "I'll give you the stories and you can put it all together and write the book." He departed just a few months later after I'd received not nearly enough from him. We did have several great phone calls though and laughed anew at some of the episodes and characters featured in what I've turned into these two books.

Thanks mate you inspired me and gave me the impetus to get cracking. You were never one to let the facts get in the way of a good story so, in the interests of ending up with a book that more closely reflects the truth, maybe it has turned out better this way.

Lastly I must again thank my partner Robyn who has indulged and fed me while I've laboured at my computer these many months. Thank you my love.

www.ingramcontent.com/pod-product-compliance
Lightning Source LLC
Chambersburg PA
CBHW072002290426
44109CB00018B/2102